P9-DWI-835

A Sustainable Life

Quaker Faith and Practice in the Renewal of Creation

by Douglas Gwyn

foreword by Steve Chase

FGC

QUAKERPRESS PHILADELPHIA, PA

Copyright © 2014 by Douglas Gwyn

All rights reserved.

QuakerPress of Friends General Conference
1216 Arch Street, 2B
Philadelphia, PA 19107

Printed in the United States of America

Composition and design by David Botwinik

ISBN 978-1-937768-55-3 (paperback)
    978-1-937768-56-0 (digital)

Library of Congress Cataloging-in-Publication Data
Gwyn, Douglas, 1948–
    A sustainable life : quaker faith and practice in the renewal of creation / by
Douglas Gwyn ; Introduction by Steve Chase.
        pages cm
        ISBN 978-1-937768-55-3 – ISBN 978-1-937768-56-0
        1. Human ecology–Religious aspects–Society of Friends. 2. Society of
Friends–Doctrines. 3. Christian life–Quaker authors. I. Title.
    BX7731.3.G86 2014
    248.4'896–dc23
                    2014015225

The scripture quotations contained herein (unless otherwise specified) are from
the New Revised Standard Version Bible copyright © 1989 by the Division of
Christian Education of the National Council of Churches of Christ in the U.S.A.
Used by permission. All rights reserved.

To order more copies of this publication or other Quaker titles call
1-800-966-4556 or see the online catalog at www.quakerbooks.org.

CONTENTS

FOREWORD
Answering The Kabarak Call

"Seek first the Kingdom of God." This radical notion, lived out in the midst of a world marred by empire and oppression, was the core conviction of prophetic Judaism and the Jewish renewal movement led by Jesus in first-century Palestine. It was also the core conviction of the friends and followers of Jesus who were derisively called "Quakers" during the mid-1600s in England. For these early Quakers, being faithful meant attending to the inward motion of Divine Wisdom in their hearts and the outward motion of waging a nonviolent "Lamb's War" in their communities to build up the "Peaceable Kingdom." It meant doing all they could, even in the face of government repression, to foster an alternative way of life that leaves behind the lust for power, profits, and prestige, and embodies a deep love of God, neighbors, and all creation.

Few Quaker scholars have focused more on the nonviolent revolutionary faith and practice of early Quakers than Doug Gwyn. I was therefore pleased to end up standing next to him one night in the dinner line at Pendle Hill, the Quaker study center where Gwyn teaches. This chance meeting gave me the opportunity to thank him for his ministry in such books as *Apocalypse of the Word: The Life and Message of George Fox*, *The Covenant Crucified: Quakers and the Beginnings of Capitalism*, and *Seekers Found: Atonement in Early Quaker Experience*. I was grateful to Gwyn because these books are among the ones that have shaped and reshaped my own faith and practice. They have repeatedly reminded me that the inward and outward breath of the Quaker movement is revelation and revolution. Not one or the other, but both. It makes no sense to just breathe in and it makes no sense to just breathe out.

In this core insight, Gwyn and I are not alone. When I became a Quaker in 1968 at the age of thirteen, I got to know many other

Quakers who were attracted to the mystical and prophetic spiritual vision of early Friends. While the language of the Kingdom of God was not all that common among the radical Quakers I knew back then, we did resonate deeply with Martin Luther King's prophetic call for people of faith and goodwill to join together with our neighbors and build up what King called the "Beloved Community." Those of us who knew a little Quaker history clearly recognized that this was just a more modern expression of what the early Quakers meant when they talked about waging the Lamb's War for the Peaceable Kingdom of God.

The ongoing need for the "nonviolent revolution of values" called for by King has only become more pressing in the years since he was assassinated. Gwyn goes at this truth head on. In this new book, *A Sustainable Life: Quaker Faith and Practice in the Renewal of Creation*, Gwyn argues that we are living in what may be the "end times" of a global, corporate, industrial-capitalist civilization that enchants and deludes, as well as oppresses and destroys. As he wisely notes in this book:

> The "end of the world" has become not just an imminent threat but an unfolding tragedy. Resource depletion, environmental degradation, population pressures, accelerating species extinctions and climate change — combined with the ruthless exploitation of large sectors of humanity through global capitalist expansion and the chronic state of war required to maintain that system — are ending the world day by day. We who live in enclaves of wealth and privilege ignore this reality only through a denial as systematic and vehement as the system itself.

This is the stark reality that has inspired the little book you hold in your hands, a book that encourages a radical renewal of contemporary Quaker faith and practice in light of the sustainability crisis. This stark reality is also inspiring Quakers all around the world to return to our prophetic roots. As Gwyn notes, "The Society of Friends today continues to attract many whose hearts hunger and thirst for peace, justice, and a sustainable world." I would go one step further and say that the spirit of revolutionary faithfulness may actually be intensifying among us today.

To catch a glimpse of this possibility one only has to read the *Kabarak Call for Peace and Ecojustice*, which was approved and sent out to Friends everywhere by attendees at the Sixth World Conference of Friends held in April 2012 at Kabarak University in Kenya. This was the largest and most diverse World Conference of Friends in history, and the participants gathered together to listen carefully to the small, still voice of God and to each other.

Their revelation was powerful. Sounding like the prophet Hosea by the end of the conference, they ultimately blasted through their lingering denial and complacency about the state of the world and our souls. As these Friends put it, it is time to face some hard truths about the extent and impact of organized sin in our world:

> We have heard of the disappearing snows of Kilimanjaro and glaciers of Bolivia, from which come life-giving waters. We have heard appeals from peoples of the Arctic, Asia and Pacific. We have heard of forests cut down, seasons disrupted, wildlife dying, of land hunger in Africa, of new diseases, droughts, floods, fires, famine and desperate migrations – this climatic chaos is now worsening. There are wars and rumors of war, job loss, inequality and violence. We fear our neighbors. We waste our children's heritage. All of these are driven by our dominant economic systems – by greed not need, by worship of the market, by Mammon and Caesar. Is this how Jesus showed us to live?

These Friends answered with a simple no, and then made an even bolder move. Not content to reject the worldly sins of domination, denial, and distraction, they also rejected the worldly counsel of despair and inaction. Echoing the first psalm that says, "happy are those who do not follow the advice of the wicked ... or sit in the seat of scoffers," these Quakers urged Friends everywhere to become ever more faithful and joyful nonviolent revolutionaries in our personal, professional, and public lives. As the Kabarak statement declares, "We are called to work for the peaceable Kingdom of God on the whole earth, in right sharing with all peoples." This is not trivial. This statement probably matters more than we currently know.

I first learned of the *Kabarak Call For Peace and Ecojustice* when two members of Putney Friends Meeting in Vermont came back from Kenya and shared their experiences with members of our meeting. Rosemary Zimmerman, one of the co-clerks of the Young Adult Friends group at the conference, shared her excitement about spending a week in Kenya with over 850 Quakers who came from Asia, Africa, the Middle East, Europe, Latin America, and North America. She also talked movingly of the racial, theological, and class diversity at the gathering. At the same time, she reported that this deep diversity of experience and belief frequently led to misunderstandings and division. To her heartbreak and disappointment, the Young Adult Friends group could not even agree on the wording of a short epistle to the rest of the gathering. She felt torn and even somewhat wounded by the gathering's human brokenness.

Noah Baker Merrill, who had given a sermon at the gathering on behalf of North American Friends, also shared his personal experiences with us. He started by agreeing with Rosemary, even offering some additional examples of the painful conflicts that he witnessed at the gathering. Yet, Noah also said that this brokenness was not the only truth of the gathering. For all their difficulties, and sometime antagonisms, the Friends at this world gathering ultimately came together in love and approved the *Kabarak Call For Peace and Ecojustice* by unanimous consent.

According to Noah, the *Call* is nothing less than a miracle and one of the most powerful statements of modern Quaker faith and practice that he has ever heard. He said he wanted us to hear it word for word and asked if I would read the *Call* out loud to the members of our meeting. Noah urged everyone to listen carefully — as if this message were being spoken as ministry in one of our most "gathered" meetings for worship.

I took Noah's copy, allowed some time for us to settle into silence, and then finally stood up and started reading to everyone in our fellowship room. It was not long before I was crying and shaking as I spoke. For me, the tears did not flow because of the bad news mentioned early in the *Call*. My tears flowed because of the good news of who we could become with God's help. Choked up, I read the following words to my spiritual community:

- *We are called to see what love can do: to love our neighbor as ourselves, to aid the widow and orphan, to comfort the afflicted and afflict the comfortable, to appeal to consciences and bind the wounds.*

- *We are called to teach our children right relationship, to live in harmony with each other and all living beings in the earth, waters and sky of our Creator, who asks, "Where were you when I laid the foundations of the world?" (Job 38:4)*

- *We are called to do justice to all and walk humbly with our God, to cooperate lovingly with all who share our hopes for the future of the earth.*

- *We are called to be patterns and examples in a 21st century campaign for peace and ecojustice, as difficult and decisive as the 18th and 19th century drive to abolish slavery.*

I then came to the final words of the Kabarak Call, which broke me open even more.

We dedicate ourselves to let the living waters flow through us — where we live, regionally, and in wider world fellowship. We dedicate ourselves to building the peace that passeth all understanding, to the repair of the world, opening our lives to the Light to guide us in each small step.

Finishing the statement, I sat down and we settled into worshipful silence to let these words find their way into our hearts. By this time, I was not the only one crying.

My meeting was profoundly inspired by the *Call*. We endorsed the statement as our own guide to the future at a business meeting, and we are still exploring how to move into this more faithful way of life together. We are now consciously seeking, and experimenting with ways to answer the *Kabarak Call* as a spiritual community.

This is not an easy journey of discernment for most of us. There is no quick fix book available called *Five Easy Ways to Be Faithful to God – and Foster a Beloved Community*. Such a book would also not likely help us, even if it existed. To answer the *Kabarak Call* meaningfully, our meeting is coming to recognize that we need to move beyond any illusive desire for a quick and easy fix to our often disordered spiritual lives. As Gwyn notes, "The Religious Society of Friends, at least in North America and Britain, is firmly embedded in a white, middle-class frame of reference and unsustainable habits of consumption." While many of us have, in John Woolman's words, wisely rejected "oppression in the extreme" that "appears terrible," we are still frequently, and often profoundly, complicit in many widely accepted patterns of "oppression in more refined appearances."

Doug Gwyn gets this, too. In the preface of this book, he shares this difficult, but liberating, truth with us.

> *Sustainability is not just one more concern to add to our others, but the framework in which Friends today must contemplate, even rethink, every aspect of our Quaker faith and practice: personal spirituality, worship and ministry, our social testimonies and work for peace and justice, our processes of personal and group discernment, our history, everything. We all have concern today for Quaker renewal. But Quaker renewal is predicated upon renewal of God's creation on this planet. To withdraw further into enclaves of economic privilege and oases of protected environments, while the unfolding crisis ravages wide swaths of the planet, is not renewal but captivity.*

I am glad to be able to recommend that my meeting read Doug Gwyn's new book together and use our discussion of it to reflect on our own journey to greater faithfulness and liberation as a spiritual community. I also recommend this book to you and your meeting. *A Sustainable Life: Quaker Faith and Practice in the Renewal of Creation* helps us face some hard truths about the multidimensional crisis that modern life has become, but it also returns our attention to our common Inward Teacher; to a renewed understanding of our faith tradition's historic scriptures; and to inspiring examples of faithfulness in the history of prophetic Judaism, the early Jesus movement, and the Quaker movement. This book, using these spiritual resources, opens up a contemporary path toward answering the *Kabarak Call* with greater faithfulness to our historic testimony of integrity, simplicity, community, justice, non-violent resistance, and, as George Fox put it so long ago, living "in unity with Creation."

Welcome to Doug Gwyn's inspired and thoughtful new book. Welcome to revelation, repentance, and revolution. Welcome to a sustainable spiritual life beyond denial, distraction, and despair that puts its "shoulder to the wheel" of nurturing the Beloved Community and the renewal of Creation. Welcome to a renewed sense of joy and living adventurously no matter what the outcome. Welcome to the possibility that the outcome might be better than we often allow ourselves to believe. Welcome to the Quaker way at its best and most powerful.

Steve Chase
March 2014

Steve Chase is a member of Putney Friends Meeting in Vermont, the author of *Letters To A Fellow Seeker: A Short Introduction To The Quaker Way*, and the director of Antioch University New England's masters program in Advocacy for Social Justice and Sustainability.

PREFACE

This is a book I have intended to write for forty years. It just took me that long to live into it.

Following an experience of calling to ministry in 1968, I finished an undergraduate degree in zoology and enrolled at Union Theological Seminary in New York in 1971. As my biblical and theological studies progressed, I felt a strong conviction that someday I must try to synthesize my scientific training with my theological studies, in order to honor my deep sense of spiritual connection with the earth and to contribute to the environmental movement just underway at that time. In particular, I found the apocalyptic literature of the Bible, bizarre as it seems to many, to be crucial. It is the stream of ancient Hebrew and Christian prophetic faith that brings the whole of creation, the natural world, into the scope of God's redemptive work in history.

Recent scholarship on biblical apocalyptic thought also informed my reading of George Fox and early Friends, which led to my first book, *Apocalypse of the Word: The Life and Message of George Fox* (1986). That led on to further study of the political and economic meaning of early Quaker revolutionary witness, in *The Covenant Crucified: Quakers and the Beginnings of Capitalism* (1995). I completed a trilogy on early Friends with an exploration of the ways radical religion and politics converged in the spirituality of the Quaker movement in *Seekers Found: Atonement in Early Quaker Experience* (2000). In each case, my training in biblical theology, at Union Seminary and then at Drew University, helped me read the "code" of early Quaker writings in ways that most historians had not done.

Along the way, in each book, I pointed briefly to the spiritual sensitivity to the natural world among early Friends, especially in Fox's writings. But their conflict with the Puritan and Restoration establishments of seventeenth-century England shifted early

Quaker focus and energies of early Friends in other directions. My studies followed those developments.

With *Conversation with Christ: Quaker Meditations on the Gospel of John* (2011), I began to present early Quaker biblical insights without the "baggage" of seventeenth-century history, which many find burdensome. The book has struck a chord for many Friends hungry to engage with scripture in a living way. I have also worked on a book (forthcoming) about Pendle Hill's[1] eight decades, which has further attuned my writing to contemporary issues. Now this book continues that shift in my writing ministry.

It is important to realize that the early Christian and early Quaker movements arose out of a collective sense of crisis. They were fresh syntheses of spiritual energies, religious ideas, political ferment, and social concern that spoke with prophetic power to their times. Our world today is replete with many crises. But surely the overarching crisis of our time is the rapidly escalating human impact on the life-giving balances of the earth. The crisis is not impending but unfolding. Climate change, species extinction, various tipping points with regard to natural resources, and other imbalances are already at disastrous proportions. The pressing question of our day is, how can humans (all of us, not just a few) live in a sustainable way on the earth? And how can Friends be part of that sustainable future?

The thesis of this book is that sustainability is not just one more concern among many, but the framework in which Friends today must contemplate, even rethink, every aspect of our Quaker faith and practice. We all have a concern today for Quaker renewal. But any sustainable Quaker renewal must be predicated upon renewal of God's creation on this planet. To withdraw further into enclaves of economic privilege and oases of protected environments, while the unfolding crisis ravages wide swaths of the planet, is not renewal but captivity.

The chapters of this book grew out of teaching at Pendle Hill, the Quaker center for study and contemplation near Philadelphia. I am grateful to the Young Adult Leadership Development group of summer 2011, who patiently helped me find my way out of the seventeenth century, and to the Quaker Faith and Practice class in the fall term of 2011, among whom the thesis of this book began to gel. I am also grateful to the Woodbrooke Quaker Study Centre in Birmingham, England, for the opportunity to serve for three months as a Friend in Residence in the spring of 2012. The drafting of these chapters took place there, between stints of practical assistance to visitors and staff. The Quaker Faith and Practice class during the fall term of 2012 responded helpfully to the draft chapters and encouraged me on. I also thank Brian Drayton, botanist and esteemed minister among New England Friends, for his feedback on chapters. Finally, I thank Chel Avery and Barbara Mays for their insightful editing and shepherding the manuscript to publication.

As with all my writing, readers will have to abide with a certain experimental quality here. My intention is to invite and to provoke the "prophetic imagination" of Friends, not to write safe books that reflect scholarly consensus or reassure Friends in what they already know and believe. These are times that call us urgently to reconsider and reinvest. So please excuse any points where I may have overgeneralized in the interest of brevity or overstated the vision that compels me.

In citing early Quaker writings, I have noted where the original texts can be found in books currently in print and relatively easy to find, if readers wish to read more. Often this has meant directing readers to my own books, where I quote from Quaker literature long out of print and available only in research libraries.

The exposition of Quaker faith and practice in this book focuses on overall structure, dynamic interactions, and abiding paradoxes. This approach probably makes this book less a starting place for seekers and new Friends than a guide for Friends in reframing their faith and practice. The aim is to help readers recognize a working whole, rather than lists of things Friends believe and do. Any hope of a sustainable life in the twenty-first century must proceed from a sense of the whole.

Douglas Gwyn

Pendle Hill, Spring 2014

INTRODUCTION

This book has grown out of a course in Quaker faith and practice I taught at Pendle Hill, the Quaker center for study and contemplation near Philadelphia, during the autumn terms of 2011, 2012, and 2013. Teaching at Pendle Hill aims to educate the whole person, by immersing student and teacher alike in the communal rhythms of daily worship, manual work, and personal study. In that context, a course on Quaker thought and history does not remain abstract but integrates with mind, body, and spirit. That has been the educational philosophy of Pendle Hill for more than eighty years. But through the decades, Pendle Hill has felt a growing concern for earth care, stewardship, and sustainability. Today, the practice of local sourcing of organic food for the kitchen, and a "permaculture" strategy for the preservation and use of its twenty-three acres, have placed work, study, and worship within a new horizon.

Friends in general today are living into a new era, where Quaker faith and practice must be reframed in terms of a sustainable life on this planet. Over the past three and a half centuries, Friends have conceived our faith and practice variously in terms of social revolution, religious community, peace making, holiness, social justice, personal salvation, seeking, mystical oneness, and so on. Each in its own way has been a valid and fruitful expression of Quaker witness. However, given the current crisis in the earth's vital balances and limited resources, all these frames must today find their place within a final horizon of sustainability — personal, social, and environmental. The purpose of this book is not to convince readers that there is a problem. Anyone who has paid attention in recent decades knows the depths of our crisis. Our salvation (which is not too strong a word, given our situation) is inextricably tied to the destiny of God's creation. How then shall we live? What are the spiritual foundations for a sustainable human life among the other species and within the life-sustaining balances of the earth? This book explores what might be called *deep sustainability*, an integrative vision of Quaker faith and practice in the twenty-first century. From this perspective, sustainability is not simply another new thing Friends are concerned about. It's *everything* we are about.

This concern was by no means absent from the faith and practice of early Friends in seventeenth-century England. Standing still together in the light, they experienced a new creation beginning within and among them. They also found their experience confirmed in the Bible's ancient witness. They understood their experience as Christ rebuilding their lives and renewing the creation through their concrete, daily actions — as individuals, families, workers, and consumers.

Re-reading the witness of early and traditional Friends within the horizon of the current crisis and our search for a sustainable life, we can hear a proto-environmental awareness and ethic. We can learn from past generations of Friends as we experience, experiment, and renew Quaker faith and practice for our times. In particular, George Fox's story of his early years speaks with clarity about how his experience in the light re-connected him with the earth and how he understood his experience in terms of the biblical drama of creation and redemption.

The Early Experiences of George Fox

Growing up in the Leicester village of Fenny Drayton in the 1630s, young George Fox had a sense of connection with the earth and a rightness of life that many of us enjoy in childhood. His *Journal* witnesses,

> *When I came to eleven years of age, I knew pureness and righteousness; for while I was a child I was taught how to walk and to be kept pure. The Lord taught me to be faithful in all things, and to act faithfully two ways, viz. inwardly to God and outwardly to man, and to keep to "yea" and "nay" in all things. For the Lord showed me that though the people of the world have mouths full of deceit and changeable words, yet I was to keep to the "yea" and "nay" in all things; and that my*

*words should be few and savoury, seasoned with grace; and
that I might not eat and drink to make myself wanton but for
health, using the creatures in their service, as servants in their
places, to the glory of him that hath created them; they being
in their covenant, and I being brought up into the covenant, as
sanctified by the Word which was in the beginning, by which
all things are upheld;wherein is unity with the creation.*

*But people being strangers to the covenant of life with
God, they eat and drink to make themselves wanton with the
creatures, devouring them upon their own lusts, and living in
all filthiness, loving foul ways and devouring the creation;
and all this in the world, in the pollutions thereof, without
God; and therefore I was to shun all such.*[1]

Young George was like many earnest young Puritans and
Seekers who converged in the Quaker movement in years to come.
He was given to intense introspection. He found his elders to be
morally lax and careless with their words. He resolved to speak less
and to be true to his word. His neighbors commented on the boy:
"If George says 'Verily,' there's no altering him."[2]

But note how George's integrity of speech and action, which
became a Quaker hallmark in years to come, also placed him in
faithful relation to the earth. He felt a covenantal relationship with
the creatures and therefore bound to consume moderately and
work with the creatures responsibly. He mentions the creatures
being "in their covenant," probably referring to God's blessing of
the creatures (Gen. 1:22)[3] and promise to preserve the creation
(Gen. 8:21-22). In years to come, Fox came to understand his covenant relationship as a "covenant of light." The light is a covenant in
that it is God's unconditional, loving presence with us, always ready
to lead, always ready to forgive and begin again. The covenant of
light is the presence of Christ, the Word who created and upholds
all things (John 1:1-4; Col. 1:15-17), alluded to by Fox above. As one
turns to the light, attends to it and learns to live according to its
leading, one lives into the covenant. Living faithfully in the light
not only leads into peaceful and just relations with other humans. It
also teaches one how to live wisely upon the earth. "Unity with the

creation" is not simply a sentiment or an empty affirmation. It is a moderate, healthy life in harmony with the earth. The Word that created all things is a light in each person that guides into unity with the creation.

Young George recognized how readily people conform and join with others in selfish and immoderate habits of consumption or to abuse fellow creatures, human or animal, in work. His avoidance of such company was less a matter of smug superiority than fear of absorbing bad habits before he had found his way into a life of integrity. He realized that people who are out of touch with the light, their inward teacher, are "strangers to the covenant," given to carelessness and excessive habits, "devouring the creation." His reference to "lusts" may be off-putting to us today, but we are well acquainted with the addictive habits of consumption that we learn from one another and from a highly commercialized, affluent society. Similarly, Fox's language of "filthiness," "foul ways" and "pollutions" sounds priggish to us today. But we are painfully aware how human consumptive habits are indeed polluting the earth, fouling the soil, water, and air, and pushing other species to misery and extinction. These physical pollutions have a spiritual and moral dimension.

Finally, Fox writes of "using the creatures in their service, as servants in their places, to the glory of him that hath created them." He probably has in mind the blessing of man and woman in Genesis 1:28 — "God blessed them, and God said to them, 'Be fruitful and multiply, and fill the earth and subdue it, and have dominion over the fish of the sea and over the birds of the air and over every living thing that moves upon the earth.'" Today we hear this blessing with misgiving. We have indeed multiplied and filled the earth, with more than six billion of us, rapidly advancing toward seven. We have indeed dominated the earth and subdued it in selfish, exploitative, and ruinous ways. But we cannot mend our ways by pretending that we are just one of the species. We have God-given abilities that increasingly dominate life on the planet, for good or for ill. The dominion God blesses and Fox understands is not about human power but divine wisdom. It is not about feeding the vainglory of human greed, but serving as God's agents, God's stewards in creation, to the glory of its Creator.

When God says in Genesis 1:26, "Let us make humankind in our image, according to our likeness," who does God address? In the story thus far, only God and the cosmos have appeared. Can it be that God speaks to the entire creation, inviting that stupendous panoply to collaborate in creating humans? We indeed bear the image of the universe in our bodies. We are literally "stardust," formed from the elemental wreckage of a star that died billions of years ago. Adam, literally "dust," is the child of the universe. We bear witness in our bodies to the laws of thermodynamics. The genetic inheritance of life on earth is encoded in us. Yet we also bear the image of a divine origin and destiny. The image of God is manifest in our sense of a reality beyond ourselves, beyond everything we know, and in our longing for it. We yearn toward God as a plant leans to the light. The image of God is "that of God," the light that is life itself in all men and women (John 1:4, 9). Thus, to live with integrity and universal love is to honor both our mother and our father (see Exod. 20:12), the divine and the cosmos. It is to live gently upon the earth, peacefully with our fellow humans, and faithfully to the knowledge of God in us.

But like many of us, as he moved through adolescence, George Fox was jarred from his sense of innocence, connection with nature, and personal integrity. In 1643, at age nineteen, the troubled young man left home. "The Lord . . . said to me, 'Thou seest how young people go together into vanity and old people into the earth; and thou must forsake all, both young and old, and keep out of all, and be as a stranger to all.'"[4]

He was like thousands of other young Seekers in the mid-1640s. With a civil war raging and many different Christian teachings competing against each other, these ardent young souls dropped out of all religion, looking for something authentic and transformative. Like some other young Seekers, Fox found some solace alone with nature.

> *My troubles continued, and I was often under great temptations; and I fasted much, and walked abroad in solitary places many days, and often took my Bible and went and sat in hollow trees and lonesome places till night came on; and*

frequently in the night walked mournfully about by myself, for I was a man of sorrows in the times of the first workings of the Lord in me.[5]

Young Fox read and listened to many teachers but joined with none of the churches, either traditional or experimental:

For I saw there was none among them all that could speak to my condition. And when all my hopes in them and in all men were gone, so that I had nothing outwardly to help me, nor could tell what to do, then, Oh then, I heard a voice which said, "There is one, even Christ Jesus, that can speak to thy condition," and when I heard it my heart did leap for joy. . . . My desires after the Lord grew stronger, and zeal in the pure knowledge of God and of Christ alone, without the help of any man, book, or writing. . . . And then the Lord did gently lead me along, and did let me see his love, which was endless and eternal . . . and that love let me see myself as I was without him. And I was afraid of all company, for I saw them perfectly where they were, through the love of God which let me see myself.[6]

Thus, by early 1647, now aged twenty-two, Fox began to know more distinctly the love and guidance of God that he had known more instinctively as a child. He began to see himself "as I was without him." That is, he began to see himself from a new place within. He could see how he had been when he felt lost and bereft of God. He was still wary of human society, which he feared would draw him back into confusion. But he began to see others in the same love that helped him see himself more clearly.

This was no quick fix. At times,

My troubles, my sorrows, and my temptations were so great, that I thought many times I should have despaired, I was so tempted. But when Christ opened to me how he was tempted by the same Devil and had overcome him and bruised his head [Gen. 3:15], that through him and his power, light, grace and spirit, I should overcome also, I had confidence in him.

And I found that there were two thirsts in me, the one after the creatures, to have gotten help and strength there, and the

other after the Lord the creator and his Son Jesus Christ. And
I saw all the world could do me no good. If I had a king's diet,
palace, and attendants, all would have been as nothing, for
nothing gave me comfort but the Lord by his power. And I saw
professors [i.e., confessing Christians], priests, and people
were whole and at ease in a condition that was my misery,
and loved that which I would have been rid of. But the Lord
did stay my desires upon himself, from whom my help came,
and my care was cast upon him alone.[7]

Thus, both the light of Christ within and the example of Christ in the gospels helped him weather temptations. He gained "confidence," faith, in Christ as one who had suffered temptation and overcome. He also learned that his desires for "creatures" — people and things — could never be satisfied, even if he had everything he wanted. The Lord alone could satisfy his deepest existential yearning and place all lesser needs and desires in perspective.

In the following months of 1647, as Fox steadfastly remained in that teachable place of the Spirit, his discernment deepened.

Then after this there did a pure fire appear in me . . . and then
the spiritual discerning came to me, by which I did discern my
own thoughts, groans and sighs, and what it was that did veil
me, and what it was that did open me. And that which could
not abide in the patience nor endure the fire, in the Light I
found to be the groans of the flesh which had veiled me and
that could not be patient in all trials. And I discovered the
groans of the spirit, which did open me, and made interces-
sion to God, in which spirit is the true waiting upon God for
redemption of the body and of the whole creation.[8]

Wordless sighing and groaning out of the silence were sometimes features of earliest Quaker worship. Like Fox, early Friends struggled to give themselves over completely to the life, power and will of God. But not all groans are the same. Some groaning is impatient and some groaning is patient, the work of God's Spirit to liberate us from captivity. Early Friends remembered the story of the Exodus. When the children of Israel groaned in their Egyptian bondage, God began acting to liberate them (Exod. 2:23-25; 3:7-8). But Fox also draws here upon Paul's words in Romans 8:19-25, which draw the rest of creation into the drama of God's redemptive work in Christ. Paul testifies that

> *the creation waits with eager longing for the revealing of the children of God; for the creation was subjected to futility, not of its own will but by the will of the one who subjected it, in hope that the creation itself will be set free from its bondage to decay and obtain the freedom of the glory of the children of God. We know that the whole creation has been groaning in labor pains until now; and not only the creation, but we ourselves, who have the first fruits of the Spirit, groan inwardly while we wait for adoption, the redemption of our bodies.*

With "bondage to decay," Paul probably refers to the ancient Stoic idea of what today we would call the law of entropy. Things fall apart: life gives way to death; the universe itself winds down or collapses at some point.

But "subjected to futility" probably refers to the Hebrew sense that human dominion over creation (recall Gen. 1:26-28) goes awry as humans abandon the counsel of God to pursue their own ideas and interests (Gen. 3). Even in Paul's ancient time, there was a sense that God's stewards were plundering the treasury of creation, mismanaging and wrecking its beauty. Today the folly and futility of human power over creation is much more blatantly obvious. Creation's hope lies in the emergence of God's children, men and women who, as Fox writes, are willing to let their false thirsts and groans die by the power of the Cross (synonymous for Fox with the light within), that the true child of God may live within us and redeem not only our bodies but the whole creation (or at least our infinitesimal corner of it on this planet).

So young George Fox saw more than his own eternal reward at stake in his spiritual struggle. He groaned and strove within himself for a present life of integrity and an overcoming power that few Christians around him imagined possible, much less attempted to find. They felt "whole and at ease" in alienation from the real transforming power of the light. More than that, he saw the destiny of creation intimately connected to the way he waited patiently upon the Lord and lived out his daily existence in the body. And still more, he felt the whole of creation in his body. He experienced the vivid, apocalyptic images of the Hebrew and early Christian prophets being fulfilled in his own experience.

> *I saw the mountains burning up and the rubbish, and the rough and crooked ways and places made smooth and plain that the Lord might come into his tabernacle [Isa. 40:3-4]. These things are to be found in man's heart. But to speak of these things being within seemed strange to the rough and crooked and mountainous ones. Yet the Lord said, "O Earth, hear the word of the Lord!"*[9]

Fox uses the prophecy of Isaiah to speak of his experience of being re-created in the power of the Spirit. His "ups and downs" are smoothed out, the needless or inappropriate "rubbish" of false desires and vain pastimes burned away. He is becoming the remarkably resilient and focused person that will speak truth fearlessly over the next forty years, in the face of violent mobs and harsh imprisonments. Again, Fox's use of Isaiah's prophecy is more than figures of speech. He finds in his embodied spiritual transformation a microcosm of a larger renewal of creation. This personal transformation is the "revealing of the children of God" the creation awaits with eager longing. As Walter Wink writes, we are the "missing link" between the apes and the fully realized humanity we were created to become.[10]

By 1648, at age 24, this new creation was coming into fullness in young Fox. He witnesses,

> *Now was I come up in spirit through the flaming sword into the paradise of God. All things were new, and all the creation gave another smell unto me than before, beyond what words can utter. I knew nothing but pureness, and innocency, and righteousness, being renewed up into the image of God by Christ Jesus, so that I say I was come up to the state of Adam which he was in before he fell. The creation was opened to me, and it was showed me how all things had their names given*

them according to their nature and virtue. . . . Great things did the Lord lead me into, and wonderful depths were opened unto me, beyond what can by words be declared; but as people come into subjection to the spirit of God, and grow up in the image and power of the Almighty, they may receive the Word of wisdom, that opens all things, and come to know the hidden unity of the Eternal Being.[11]

The sense of smell Fox mentions here, even if it is only metaphorical, indicates how embodied the transformation is. Having passed through the fire of his own transformation, he saw the primal purity of nature restored. He saw into the "nature and virtue" – the essence and usefulness – of the creatures. The "names" of the creatures refers to the story of God letting Adam name the animals (Gen. 2:19-20) in some pure language before the corruption of language at Babel (Gen. 11).

Divine insight into nature is "beyond what words can utter," or at least in any speech we share. But Fox had gone past language in the "groans too deep for words" and silent waiting of the worship groups he was establishing in the Midlands in the latter 1640s. The "Word of wisdom" that created all things also opens their nature to the single eye, which finds them all in "the hidden unity of the Eternal Being." But also notice that Fox is not content to be a mystic, with his own special revelations. He emphasizes that these insights and this state of being are available to anyone who will "come into subjection to the spirit of God, and grow up in the image and power of the Almighty." The rest of his life was devoted to guiding others to the source of that power.

At this time Fox was "at a stand in my mind whether I should practice physic for the good of mankind, seeing the nature and virtues of the creatures were so opened to me by the Lord."[12] Indeed, Fox did practice herbal medicine in the years to come. But his main activity was in the ministry of turning others to the same light that had transformed him. He had further insight at this time into

those three great professions of the world, physic, divinity (so called), and law. . . . [T]hese three, the physicians, the priests, and the lawyers, ruled the world . . . the one pretending the cure of the body, the other the cure of the soul, and the third the property of the people. But I saw they were all out, out of the wisdom, out of the faith, out of the equity and perfect law of God. And as the Lord opened these things unto me, I felt his power went forth over all, by which all might be reformed, if they would receive and bow unto it.[13]

So Fox's vision was not narrowly "religious." He did not set out to found a new sect. He had discovered the key to a radical reformation of all society. Besides his ministry and his avocation as an herbalist, he was also an advocate of English legal reform, the liquidation of church properties to empower the poor, and other socio-economic reforms. In these early years, working as a shoemaker, he lived very simply and often gave his money away to beggars and needy people. He advocated to local justices for fair wages for seasonal farm workers. But all true personal and social transformation must proceed from the wisdom of God, revealed by the light, or seed, within.

The trembling in worship that earned early Friends the epithet "Quakers" probably began in 1648. Fox recalls that year,

As I was sitting in a Friend's house in Nottinghamshire . . . I saw there was a great crack to go throughout the earth, and a great smoke to go as the crack went; and that after the crack there should be a great shaking. This was the earth in people's hearts, which was to be shaken before the Seed of God was raised out of the earth. And it was so; for the Lord's power began to shake them, and great meetings we began to have.[14]

Fox finds the earthquakes envisioned in Revelation (6:12; 16:18) fulfilled in his own body and the bodies of others in these early worship groups. The "earth" in the heart is the ego-driven sense of self that views other humans and the creation itself as resources to be exploited. This way of being doesn't let go easily, as Fox's spiritual journey has suggested. It must be shaken and broken open for the "Seed" to be raised within. Fox understands this seed to be Christ, the seed of the woman (again, Gen. 3:15) who overcomes the tempter. Christ is also the seed of Abraham, in whom all the peoples of the earth are blessed (Gen. 12:3). In both cases, the seed is a *universal* gift, a presence and blessing in all peoples in all ages. But the seed of Abraham also connotes *peoplehood*, gathered community with a calling to communicate through word and deed God's love and wisdom to others. Fox's ministry was about gathering that transformative people.

The seed is another name for the light within. Light and seed are two central metaphors in the writings of Fox and another key early leader, Isaac Penington. Seed and light are two aspects of the same reality. Seed language is more about *being* and *willing*, light is more about *knowing* and *doing*. Both light and seed are words for God's presence with us — in Hebrew, *Emmanuel* — not only for our own redemption into wholeness/holiness, but also in order that we may become agents of healing wholeness to others, in society and throughout the creation.

Accordingly, as his transformation moved to completion in 1648, Fox was called to his great life vocation:

> *The Lord commanded me to go abroad into the world, which was like a briery, thorny wilderness, and when I came in the Lord's mighty power with the word of life into the world, the world swelled and made a noise like the great raging waves of the sea. Priests and professors, magistrates and people, were all like a sea, when I came to proclaim the day of the Lord amongst them and to preach repentance to them.*[15]

In contrast to the paradise of Eden that Fox has entered, the world is a "briery, thorny wilderness." When Adam and Eve are cast out from Eden and its entrance is blocked by a fiery sword, they no longer experience the earth as a paradise. Adam sweats, both from labor and from anxiety, to derive sustenance from the earth, which yields thorns and thistles. Eve's life is suspended between the patriarchal rule of Adam and the mortal terror of childbirth (Gen. 3:16-19). Living as strangers to the covenant of light, men and women create among themselves a world of struggle, anxiety, domination, and strife. Fox must preach repentance to them; that is, a decisive *turn* to the light and source of life and peace within them.

But the response he receives is rage. People are offended that he so radically confronts their practice of religion, their morality and social norms, their treatment of the other creatures of the earth. He compares them to the raging waves of the sea, which in the Bible often serve as an image of chaos. Without the light's guidance, human society is a barely managed chaos that routinely boils over into violence between people, between nations, and upon the rest of creation. Following the Gospel of John, Fox contrasts "world" with God's creation. The world is the distorted realm of human perceptions, interests, and prejudices. God created the earth. The world is what we "make" of it. "World" of course includes many accurate human perceptions, good motives, and virtuous actions. But the sheer jumble of human activity is a chaotic realm.

As we saw earlier, Fox had experienced the mountains laid low, the valleys lifted up, and the crooked ways made smooth for Christ's coming within. That experience led him to resist social hierarchy of all kinds:

> Moreover when the Lord sent me forth into the world, he forbade me to put off my hat to any, high or low; and I was required to "thee" and "thou" all men and women, without any respect to rich or poor, great or small. . . . I was not to bid people "good morrow" or "good evening," neither might I bow or scrape with my leg to any one; and this made the sects and professions [churches] to rage. But the Lord's power carried me over all to his glory . . . for the heavenly day of the Lord sprang from on high, and brake forth apace, by the light of which many came to see where they were. . . . And though it was but a small thing in the eye of man, yet a wonderful confusion it brought upon all professors and priests.[16]

Fox and early Friends had a genius for using seemingly minor, mundane gestures to insinuate much larger questions about social relationships. Their strange manners sparked a great deal of anger and abuse against them. But as Fox remarks, "many came to see where they were." The usual pleasantries of "have a nice day" were swept aside in order to confront men and women with "the day of the Lord," a moment of startling self-awareness and decision. It was a cathartic moment that unleashed violent rage in some and opened a new creation for others.

Fox and those who gathered with him in the next few years carried on a relentless critique against the established, state-enforced Church of England. It required people to attend their parish "steeplehouse" and support it with a tenth of their income, in order to listen to a university-trained clergyman preach and to recite creeds they didn't necessarily understand or agree with:

When I heard the bell toll to call people together to the steeplehouse, it struck at my life, for it was just like a market-bell to gather people together that the priest might set forth his ware to sale. Oh, the vast sums of money that are gotten by the trade they make of selling the Scriptures and by their preaching, from the highest bishop to the lowest priest! What one trade else in the world is comparable to it, notwithstanding the Scriptures were given forth freely, and Christ commanded his ministers to preach freely.[17]

Early Friends understood coerced religion to be a fundamental violation of human consciousness, with a deforming effect upon human spiritual and moral sense. That effect lies at the root of other personal and social problems. Fox's core message in years to come was "Christ is come to teach his people himself by his power and spirit and to bring them off all the world's ways and teachers to his own free teaching."[18] This was a message of Christ's return, not from the sky but through the light in each person's conscience. As individuals and groups turned to this free teaching, it led them into new insights, new personal morality, more egalitarian social relations, more peaceful responses to conflict, and a gentler, more caring relationship with the earth. They understood themselves to be discovering and initiating heaven on earth.

We have seen how that transformation occurred for Fox. He led others into the same experience and partnered with a gifted group of women and men to create a new kind of church — or rather, to renew what the church had started out to be in the first decades after Jesus's death. The patterns they developed in worship and ministry, spiritual nurture and group decision making, their sacramental sense of daily life as a living testimony to the Prince of Peace — all these were inspired reinventions of early Christianity as well as pregnant figures of the kingdom of heaven for an early modern world.

Quaker Faith and Practice

The Quaker faith and practice that developed in the years to come is grounded in the presence of the light within, which is common to all humanity. The light is something deeper than human reason or emotion. One "stands still in the light" at times in opposition to what reason and emotion dictate. In the light we feel the warm, unconditional love of God. In the light we feel that same love going out to other people and to all God's creatures. We come into the oneness, "the hidden unity of the Eternal Being." As we abide in the light, a practice which must be constantly deepened and renewed, our very being changes in subtle but profound ways. We begin to live the oneness. We live in *covenant faithfulness* with *God*, with *one another* and with the *earth*.

In this study we will find that all aspects of Quaker faith and practice form a set of dynamic, enlivening tensions and paradoxes. As depicted in the graphic on this book's cover, we will find the essentials of Quaker faith and practice in sixteen elements. These constellate as eight pairs, in which each element informs, qualifies, and enlivens the other. Taken together, these eight dialectical pairings describe the wholeness we feel when Friends are at our best together.

The term "faith and practice" suggests that we have some *basic convictions* that orient our attention and intention, combined with a set of *normative behaviors* (individual and group) that proceed from our convictions. But these concrete practices also feed back into the faith, refining our beliefs and intentions.

We typically call Quaker faith and practice our Quaker "spirituality." But Quaker faith and practice is both spiritual and material. It is what we do with our garbage as much as it is how we worship. It is how we interact with strangers as much as how we make decisions together in unity. The way we befriend the light within us has implications for the way in which we befriend the needy in our community and befriend the creation. And those actions will in turn affect our personal experience of the light within.

So in this model of Quaker faith and practice, each element not only interacts with its paradoxical partner, but through that interaction, each element also interacts with all the others, creating a constantly turning, redefining whole. That's hard to comprehend. But the point is less to comprehend than to move with it and sense its vitality. So let's take this one step at a time, beginning with the basic elements of Quaker spirituality, as suggested by the traditional terms "light" and "seed."

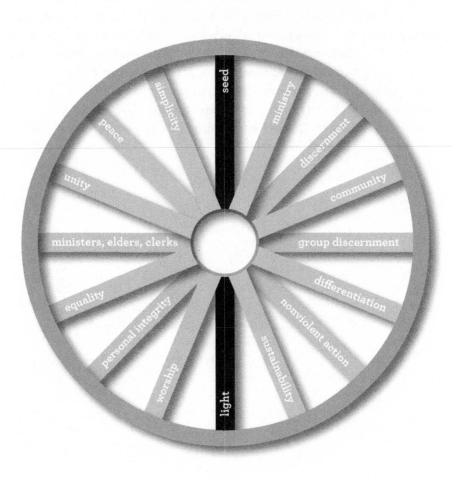

light and seed

CHAPTER 1

Quaker Spiritual Practice

The search for a sustainable life begins within. Sustained focus, intention, and effort will be required for us to embody and advocate for a human society that lives in balance with the earth. That faithful struggle will take each of us beyond our own vision, strength, even hope. To transcend burnout, cynicism, and despair we will require spiritual resources that can sustain us. But those resources are found in a direction opposite to where we usually think to look. Much of our knowledge of the current environmental crisis, the blight of social injustice, and chronic warfare is mediated. That is, we learn about these things from the media. We discuss them and network with others for social action using the internet, in particular, social media. Even our search for deeper spiritual foundations is often mediated. We read about different religions and learn new spiritual techniques, for example, through books, the internet, and other out-ward resources. But ultimately, these resources only scatter our attention, intention, and energies, leaving us exhausted and lost.

Friends have traditionally insisted that our true, sustainable spiritual resource for personal and social renewal comes from an unmediated source within ourselves. Early Friends called true spiritual knowledge "immediate," but they didn't mean that it comes right away, like results from a Google search. It comes through a regular practice of waiting. That waiting begins as an impatient, toe-tapping waiting *for* something to happen, perhaps for God to answer our questions and needs. But over time, through some mysterious combination of persistence and surrender, patience develops. We learn to wait *upon* the Lord, the Presence, the Truth — in readiness to learn, to be transformed, to serve. That is the Copernican revolution that begins a sustainable life.

As we all know, sustainability is in part the discipline of recy-cling, repurposing, and reusing materials from past growing seasons and creative periods. That discipline applies to spiritual life as much as material life. This chapter explores what we can learn from early, traditional, and modern Friends about that Copernican revolution and how it can happen in our own lives. One of the traditional que-ries (questions for reflection and self-examination) among Friends reads, "Do you come to meeting for worship with heart and mind prepared?" Powerful, life-changing experiences may take place for you in Quaker worship without any preparation. But to make the most of the worship experience on a regular basis, and to go deeper in your own personal life over time, a regular spiritual practice is necessary. No one can make you do it. Indeed, no one but you can discover the kind of spiritual practice that will be most fruitful. And what is fruitful for each individual typically shifts over time. But regular spiritual practice is necessary to growth and advancement.

Sensing this need, and not finding enough guidance in their local meetings, Friends sometimes look elsewhere. They may take time occasionally at a Catholic retreat center, for example. Or they may work one-on-one with a spiritual director. Or they may find it useful to meditate with a Buddhist *sangha* (meditation group or community). These resources often prove helpful. But there are tra-ditional practices more organic to Quaker faith and practice that Friends are rediscovering and renewing.

We speak of Quakerism as a religion of "experience," but what does that mean? Is experience whatever happens to us and what-ever we make of it? Is the "light" simply a diffuse illumination of anything and everything? Quaker spiritual practice offers a way to give *focus* and *intention* to experience. It turns the half-light of any-thing and everything into deep insight into ourselves and others. It turns generalized anxiety over personal problems and the woes of the world into focused concern and action to foster wholeness.

That focus and intention are evoked by the two guiding images of early Quaker spiritual counsel: light and seed. They are two aspects of a single reality. Just as physical light has the qualities of both a particle and a wave, so "that of God" in each of us manifests in these two ways. Quaker faith and practice is lived in the dynamic relationship between light and seed, between knowing and being, between insight and action. What the light reveals to us changes the quality of our being. The seed of a new creation is "raised up" in us. We feel compelled to act differently. Likewise, as we begin to act differently, the light reveals more truth to us. We continue to grow in this dynamic interaction. Meanwhile, this new creation is grounded in the old creation. We embody it in our natural bodies. Coming into the light in a focused way replays the dawn of creation. Light and darkness are separated (Gen. 1:3-4), and the true path forward becomes clearer. Likewise, as we live into that truth, a new life with a new will grows in us.

Margaret Fell, who became a key leader and administrator of the early Quaker movement, met George Fox in 1652 and invited him to visit her local parish church. After the priest finished preaching, Fox asked for permission to speak. As Fell recalls, Fox said, "You will say, Christ saith this, and the apostles say this, but what canst thou say? Art thou a child of the light, and hast thou walked in the light, and what thou speakest, is it inwardly from God?" She sat down in her pew and wept bitterly, saying, "We are all thieves, we are all thieves; we have taken the Scriptures in words and know nothing of them in ourselves."[1] Fell suddenly realized that her faith was mediated by hearsay. Her church had settled for creeds: propositions about Christ. Fox was offering a way of participation in the life of Christ. He offered living experience, not dead words.

Note the three ways Fox describes that participation. First, there is a kind of rebirth that happens when we wait in the light, surrender to it, and become its teachable child. Second, there is walking in the light, living out its teaching and guidance in concrete, daily steps. Finally, there is speaking from light, from both the spiritual practice of waiting for its teaching and the practical steps of living it out.

The church is not alone in the tendency to lapse into unreality. It is the human condition in general. Buddhists refer to it as delusion, not-seeing. Fox observed "a dullness and drowsy heaviness upon people."[2] Whatever our religious or philosophical persuasion, we are prone to trade the truth for truisms, to cling to forms of belief and practice long after the living content has drained away for us. And today, in a highly mediated culture like ours, we habitually take for granted what we read, hear, and see through the press, television, radio, and internet.

Recall George Fox's breakthrough experience (see the Introduction). When he gave up looking for answers from books, teachers, and groups, he heard a voice that said, "There is one, even Christ Jesus, that can speak to thy condition." Fox's condition was simply one variation on the human condition we all share: delusion. This condition has many different moods and moves in many different directions. As his transformation advanced, Fox was given discernment into some of the ways we hurt ourselves and one another as we live in that basic condition of delusion. It was disturbing to feel these different distortions of God's good human creation.

> *And I cried to the Lord, saying, "Why should I be thus, seeing I was never addicted to commit those evils?" And the Lord answered that it was needful I should have a sense of all conditions, how else should I speak to all conditions; and in this I saw the infinite love of God. I saw also that there was an ocean of darkness and death, but an infinite ocean of light and love, which flowed over the ocean of darkness. And in that also I saw the infinite love of God; and I had great openings. And as I was walking . . . the Lord said unto me, "That which people do trample upon must be thy food." And as the Lord spoke he opened it to me how that people and professors did trample upon the life, even the life of Christ was trampled upon; and they fed upon words . . . and they lived in their airy notions.*[3]

The darkness of the human condition: despair, self-harm, addiction, sinful and selfish behaviors, racial prejudice, sexism, domestic violence and abuse, economic exploitation and injustice, cruelty to animals, war, and spoiling of the earth is truly like a vast ocean, overwhelmingly painful to contemplate. But in the light we also see an infinite reservoir of God's love that overflows the darkness and heals all who come to it.

However, the light is subtle. We tend to look past it, and so "trample upon" it. We expect something more grand, or something more immediately comforting and useful. We become trapped in "airy notions." But as the Word became flesh in the person of Jesus

(John 1:14), so the light is present in our bodies (John 1:9). The light is a "suffering servant" (Isa. 53) who humbly abides with us, below our lofty ideas and dearest feelings. The light dwells with us unconditionally and speaks to every condition. In order to "stand still in the light" and to stop trampling it, we have to humble ourselves, quiet our hearts and minds, wait to feel its infinite love, receive its divine wisdom, and be led into the newness of life.

Three Samples of Early Quaker Spiritual Counsel

Sarah Blackborow was a seeker who was transformed by the light soon after Friends arrived in London from the North in 1654. She wrote from her own experience to other seeking souls in A *Visit to the Spirit in Prison* (1658):

> *Wisdom hath uttered forth her voice to you, but the eye and ear which is abroad, waiting upon the sound of words without you, is that which keeps you from your Teacher within you; and this is the reason that in all your seeking you have found nothing; such as your seeking is, such is your finding. . . . Therefore . . . come out of the many things; there's but one thing needful [see Luke 10:40-42], keep to it . . . that into my Mother's house you may come, and into the chamber of her that conceived me, where you may embrace, and be embraced, of my dearly beloved one [see Song of Sol. 3:1-4]. Love is his name, Love is his nature, Love is his life.*[4]

Blackborow gently chides her readers for looking everywhere but within, for becoming lost in many things and losing the one thing. Wisdom calls from a deeper place of unworldly love. That is "the Spirit in prison" (1 Pet. 3:19) whom only we can liberate, and the only one who can liberate us. Note the mixture of feminine and masculine language for the divine presence. The divine transcends feminine and masculine, but resonates between the poles of human being in each of us.

Sarah Blackborow and early Friends spoke to a world where new religious teachings and spiritual experiments were springing up in many new directions. Our twenty-first-century world is much more awash with wisdoms, new and old, eastern and western. We easily get lost among them, sampling and experimenting, picking and combining. Each glimmers with promise, yet fails to deliver us, because we grasp mainly the "airy notions" or some rote techniques. The truth that glimmers in each remains imprisoned within us. Quaker faith and practice opens that prison door.

George Fox wrote epistles, letters that were circulated among Friends meetings, which sometimes included the kind of spiritual counsel he offered in person to individuals. This one written in 1652 is a classic example:

> *Whatever ye are addicted to, the Tempter will come in that thing; and when he can trouble you, then he gets advantage over you, and then ye are gone. Stand still in that which is pure, after ye see yourselves; and then mercy comes in. After thou seest thy thoughts, and the temptation, do not think, but submit, and then power comes. Stand still in that which shows and discovers, and there doth strength immediately come. And stand still in the Light, and submit to it, and the other will be hushed and gone; and then content[ment] comes. And when temptations and troubles appear, sink down in that which is pure, and all will be hushed and fly away. Your strength is to stand still, after ye see yourselves; whatsoever ye see yourselves addicted to . . . then ye think ye shall never overcome. And earthly reason will tell you what ye shall lose. Hearken not to that, but stand still in the Light, that shows them to you, and then strength comes from the Lord, and help, contrary to your expectation. Then ye grow up in peace, and no trouble shall move you.[5]*

Even in Fox's archaic syntax, these words probe deeply. They speak from the depth of his own experience to the depth of our experience. Words like "submit" may make us flinch and want to draw back. But remember that Fox is only asking you to submit to the light within you. Only your inward teacher can "call you out" on your favorite evasions and pet fictions about yourself.

Fox's language of "addiction" surely speaks to our contemporary condition. We live in a highly addictive culture. We participate in a consumer-driven economy, constantly harangued by commercially saturated media. Substance abuse is only the most blatant form of addiction. Even our most innocent and healthy habits may become ego attachments that leave us open to "the Tempter," who draws us into delusion. And "then ye are gone" — gone from ourselves and gone from the light. Only a stubborn practice of "standing still in the light," quieting the heart and mind, allows us to see ourselves again.

Fox's counsel is counterintuitive. It is precisely through the act of submitting to the light in stillness that clarity, strength, contentment, and will power come. Your own reason will betray you. It will invent a thousand reasons to flee. It will conjure a withering list of worries about what following this light will cost you. "Hearken not to that," Fox flatly warns. The light shows you where those fears and worries come from. If you resist them, you will find help on the way.

Twelve-step programs are very useful today for people struggling with a variety of addictions, dependencies, and codependencies. Fox's counsel comes from another age, where guiding metaphors like light and seed sufficed, without steps or techniques. It guides us through an inner landscape that techniques only trace from the outside. But like twelve-step groups, early Friends often met to encourage one another through the dark and confusing passages of the journey. We will address these group aspects of Quaker faith and practice in later chapters.

Isaac and Mary Penington were wealthy London seekers who became Friends in 1658. Isaac was already a respected minister and spiritual writer before he encountered Quakers. Educated at Cambridge, he struggled to get past his considerable intellect to find the light within. When he finally did break through, he became a helpful counselor to many. His letters are still prized among Friends today. Like Fox and other early Friends, Penington wrote of the light. But he was at his best when writing of the seed. As suggested earlier, light and seed are two aspects of the same divine presence within each of us. Light evokes the ways that presence teaches us, helps us see ourselves more clearly and discern our way forward. Seed evokes the sense of our new birth, our new being in Christ, in truth. Early Friends also used it to speak of the new will. George Fox writes of "my inward mind being joined to his good Seed" to serve God in liberating others.[6]

Some Directions to the Panting Soul (1661) contains some of Penington's classic advice to seekers of his day, who like himself had searched far and wide for a sustainable life. This passage also speaks to many of us today who lead frenetic, multi-tasking, distracted, overcommitted, and unsustainable lives.

> *Be no more than God hath made thee. Give over thine own willing; give over thine own running; give over thine own desiring to know or to be any thing, and sink down to the seed which God sows in the heart, and let that grow in thee, and be in thee, and breathe in thee, and act in thee, and thou shalt find by sweet experience that the Lord knows that, and loves and owns that, and will lead it to the inheritance of life, which is his portion. And as thou takest up the cross to thyself, and sufferest that to overspread and become a yoke over thee, thou shalt become renewed, and enjoy life, and the everlasting inheritance in that.*[7]

We heard the advice to "sink down" in Fox's counsel as well. It evokes very well the shift we feel when we stop striving, let go of ambitions and compulsions, or stop running toward this and away from that. Sinking down into God's love, new life begins to breathe and act in us. That is the life God empowers, guides, and sustains. Again, language like "the cross to thyself" and "a yoke over thee" may make some want to draw back. But it is only the true life within that we are submitting to. It is a cross in that we must abandon our sense of control and self-possession. It is a yoke in that we learn to will and to serve a love that is greater than our own. The counterintuitive truth is that here we find by "sweet experience" real joy and an authentic life of service we can sustain and which sustains us. This life is an "everlasting inheritance." It is not only sustainable through a lifetime. It is eternal: it transcends time.

The Covenant of Light

Living more consistently attuned to the light/seed, we become more faithful to a presence that abides faithfully with us. We are befriending God, who is ready to help us and heal our lives, but who respects our freedom and must be actively invited into our lives.

This is the beginning of life in the covenant, a very open-ended set of relationships that play out in three dimensions.

First, an open-ended relationship with God:

Quaker faith and practice is rooted in a living experience and deep understanding of Christ. But the light we may understand as Christ abides in people everywhere. Jews, Muslims, Buddhists, Hindus, pagans, nontheists, atheists — *all* have access to this transforming, enlightening, saving presence. They will name it with whatever terms are available and meaningful to them. Creeds are counter-productive, even to Christian faith. They turn participation in the life of God into propositions about God. Not only do creeds rule out people who don't have the "right answers," they also invite hypoc-risy when Christians mouth beliefs they don't understand or secretly doubt. So an open-ended relationship with God is partici-pation in a reality we cannot fully understand or set boundaries on.

Second, an open-ended relationship with others:

The more attuned we become to the light within ourselves, the more we recognize it in widening varieties of people. Our belief that the same light enlightens all kinds of people invites new friendships; it calls us to mutual respect and cooperation between women and men, different races, classes, and cultures. It prohibits us from resort-ing to violence — physical, verbal, emotional — to solve our conflicts. We seek to befriend the stranger, even the enemy, in the search for a peaceful life together. Friendship is a polymorphous form of rela-tionship that bridges social boundaries and subverts hierarchies of all kinds. Friendship is patient listening, waiting for the truth of the situation to emerge through dialogue. We live the covenant of light by extending friendship toward others. Widening experiences of friendship naturally lead us into community action and political advocacy to ensure the full rights and privileges of all members of society, to promote alternatives to violence, to oppose war.

Third, an open-ended relationship with the earth:

Befriending God within ourselves and "that of God in every one" is an embodied life. It is spiritual practice that locates the divine presence in our bodies. It is also material practice that leads us to live peacefully and equitably with others — and to live more simply on the earth. Quaker spiritual practice is primarily nonverbal. When we suspend language and quiet our minds, we not only become more centered in our bodies. We also feel more distinctly our relationship with the earth and its species of life. We become better stewards of God's creation, befriending the earth and its creatures. We become less "territorial" — physically, emotionally, economically, culturally, and religiously. This leads to more peaceful human relations and a less exploitative use of natural resources.

Modern Quaker Testimony

Thomas Kelly was one of the greatest Quaker poets of religious experience of modern times. His essay, "The Light Within," begins:

> *Deep within us all there is an amazing inner sanctuary of the soul, a holy place, a Divine Center, a speaking Voice, to which we may continuously return. Eternity is at our hearts, pressing upon our time-torn lives, warming us with intimations of an astounding destiny, calling us home unto Itself. Yielding to these persuasions, gladly committing ourselves in body and soul, utterly and completely, to the Light Within, is the beginning of true life. It is a dynamic center, a creative Life that presses to birth within us. It is a Light Within which illuminates the face of God and casts new shadows and new glories upon the face of men. It is a seed stirring to life if we do not choke it. It is the Shekinah of the soul, the Presence in the midst. Here is the Slumbering Christ, stirring to be awakened, to become the soul we clothe in earthly form and action. And He is within us all.*[8]

Like early Friends, Kelly evokes the divine presence through a rich variety of metaphors, rather than prescribing a series of steps of "how to get there." "There is no new technique for entrance upon this stage where the soul in its deeper levels is continuously at Home in Him."[9] He will go no further than to recommend and describe the life of continuous prayer, bringing every matter and every moment into conversation and communion with the divine. The process is difficult and frustrating at first, but becomes easier and simpler, with rewarding fruits of joy, adoration, and service. We find our hearts filled with a paradoxical combination of *contemptus mundi* and *amor mundi*. God "plucks the world out of our hearts, loosening the chains of attachment. And He hurls the world into our hearts, where we and He together carry it in infinitely tender love."[10]

Another gifted writer, William Taber, describes the presence as a living stream.

> *It is as if we have stepped into a living stream full of renewing, healing energy, a stream which reaches back and forward across time so that we are in some mysterious touch with all of those who ever have and who ever will come into the transforming Presence of the Living God and the eternal Christ. . . . Like an earthly river, this special reality seems to have no beginning and no end when we come upon it, even though we know that this stream also flows from its Source to the Eternal Ocean. Like an earthly river, it is always the same river, even though it is always alive and flowing and changing. And like an earthly river it flows between recognizable boundaries which, though they may change somewhat, still remain fundamentally the same down through the years; thus traditions and scriptures help us to know where the Stream may be found.*[11]

Patricia Loring describes Quaker spiritual practice as *listening*: "prayerful, discerning attentiveness to the Source intimated within us, evidenced through others, and discernible through the experiences of life."[12] She recommends and describes spiritual practices from a variety of traditions that can strengthen the inner life: devotional reading, journaling, various forms of meditation, prayer, visualization, icons, *lectio divina* (contemplative reading of scripture), spiritual friendships, retreats, group sharing, and simple living.

Walking is a practice common among Friends and many other people, yet rarely described. In commenting on George Fox's relentlessly itinerant ministry, often on foot, Hilary Hinds[13] reflects that walking incorporates the sense of balance we received with another's hand when we first learned to walk. That sense of balancing guidance becomes more conscious as we seek to "walk with the Lord" in our lives. Moreover, the alternation of motion between left and right legs embodies the inner dialogue that generates deep reflection.

So walking itself is an important embodied spiritual practice. Further, when we walk in open areas, where sky, trees, meadows, sea, or mountains predominate, we find ourselves in the community of species that upholds and sustains our lives at the most basic levels of existence. Certainly, it is often an experience of beauty, even grandeur. But more than that, it is an experience of community, of communion with God and with the web of life that is truly the "holy of holies."

It is often rewarding to share that experience with a friend or loved one. But it is important not to let verbal conversation intrude too much. In the realm of human language, we are cut off from the primal language the creation speaks. I personally "hear" that language most of all in the forest, that community of trees and other species that invites me into a stillness that is alive with relationship. My background in the sciences (zoology) informs me that not all is peaceful there. Competition, predation, disease, suffering, and death — as well as life, cooperation, and joy — teach me that these are all part of the web of life.

George Fox wrote of the language of creation in 1657, from his own experience:

> Such as are turned to the Light which comes from him who is the Heir of all things, which upholds all things by his word and power, these come to see how the works of the Lord praise him; his works praise him, day and night praise him, Summer and Winter praise him; Ice and Cold, and Snow praise him . . . Seed-time and Harvest praise him; and all things that are created praise him. This is the Language of them who learn of him; hear him . . . by whom all things was made, and by whom all things was created for him, and to him [see Col. 1:15-18].[14]

The life of daily devotion to the divine presence attunes us to the language of creation. It also helps us order our own lives into the chorus of praise to the creator. William Penn writes similarly that, "though God has replenished this world with abundance of good things for man's comfort, yet they are all but imperfect goods. He is the only perfect good to whom they point. But alas, men cannot see him for them; though they should always see him in them."[15] The trained inner eye finds the perfect wholeness/holiness of the divine in the passing phenomena of nature. Without that eye, we tend either to dwell mainly on the flaws of nature (including human nature) or fixate upon creatures as objects we must possess or consume. A sustainable life on the earth begins within. It retrains sense and reason.

Experiment with Light

In recent years, British Friend Rex Ambler undertook a study of George Fox's written spiritual counsel, which he compiled in *Truth of the Heart*. He also sought to distill Fox's counsel in a form more accessible to Friends and others today. Living in an era dominated by technology and technique, many today find a series of steps more helpful than the traditional Quaker palette of evocative images and metaphors. Ambler found in the "focusing" method developed by the psychologist Eugene Gendlin a helpful parallel to Fox's counsel to "stand still in the light" and Penington's guidance to "sink down to the seed." In *Light To Live By*, Ambler tells the story of his discovery and presents the guided meditations he developed from melding Fox's counsel with Gendlin's method. These include one basic meditation focusing on the individual, another for focusing on relationships, another for contemplating one's local Friends meeting or group, and one for the world. Ambler's "Experiment with Light" has engaged Friends on both sides of the Atlantic. Particularly in Britain, it has inspired the for- mation of "light groups" that meet regularly to follow the guided meditations and to share the insights gained.

The prompts of Rex Ambler's guided meditation for the indi- vidual are reproduced here.[16] Readers may wish to experiment with it for themselves, as a way to test a Quaker spiritual practice for themselves.

1. **Relax body and mind.** Start by making yourself perfectly comfortable. Feel the weight of your body on the chair (or the floor), then consciously release the tension in each part of your body. Then let all your immediate worries go, all your current preoccupations. Relax your mind so much that you give up "talking to yourself" in your head. Let yourself become wholly receptive.

2. In this receptive state of mind, **let the real concerns of your life** emerge. Ask yourself, "What is really going on in my life?" but do not try to answer the question. Let the answer come. You can be specific: "What is happening in my relationships, my work, my meeting, in my own heart and mind?" And more specifically still, ask: "Is there anything here that makes me feel uncomfortable, uneasy?" As we gradually become aware of these things, we are beginning to experience the light.

3. Now **focus on one issue** that presents itself, one thing that gives you a sense of unease. And try to get a sense of this thing as a whole. Deep down you know what it is about, but you don't normally allow yourself to take it all in and absorb the reality of it. Now is the time to do so. You don't have to get involved in this problem again, or get entangled with the feelings around it. Keep a little distance, so that you can see it clearly. Let the light show you what is really going on here. "What is it about this thing," you can ask, "that makes me feel uncomfortable?" Let the answer come. And when it does, let a word or image also come that says what it's really like, this thing that concerns you.

4. Now ask yourself **why it is like that**, or what makes it like that? Don't try to explain it. Just wait in the light till you see what it is. Let the answer come. If you get an answer like, "Because I'm afraid," or "Because that's the way she is," ask again the question why: "Why am I afraid?" "Why is she like that?" Let the full truth reveal itself, or as much truth as you are able to take at this moment. If you are really open and receptive, the answer will come.

5. When the answer comes **welcome it**. It may be painful or difficult to believe with your normal conscious mind, but if it is the truth you will recognize it immediately and realize that it is something that you need to know. Trust the light. Say yes to it. Submit to it. It will then begin to heal you. It will show you new possibilities for your life. It will show you the way through. So however bad the news seems to be at first, accept it and let its truth pervade your whole being.

6. As soon as you accept what is being revealed to you, you will begin to **feel different**. Even bad news will seem strangely good. Accepting truth about yourself is like making peace. An inner conflict is being resolved. Now there is peace. Your body may respond quite noticeably to this change. A sense of relief may make you sigh or want to laugh. Your diaphragm may heave. This is the beginning of changes that the light may bring about. But if none of this happens on this occasion do not worry. It may take longer. Notice how far you have got this time and pick it up on another occasion. In any case this is a process we do well to go through again and again, so that we can continue to grow and become more like the people we are meant to become.

When you feel ready, open your eyes, stretch your limbs, and bring the meditation to an end.

You may also wish to engage in a meditative reading of the passages quoted in this chapter from Fox, Penington, or Kelly as a way to come into the stillness and presence. In addition, the following advices and queries from Britain Yearly Meeting's *Quaker Faith & Practice*[17] offer questions and counsel that are useful at any point along one's journey.

Advices and Queries from Britain Yearly Meeting's *Quaker Faith & Practice*

#3: Bring the whole of your life under the ordering of the spirit of Christ. Are you open to the healing power of God's love? Cherish that of God within you, so that this love may grow in you and guide you. Let your worship and your daily life enrich each other. Treasure your experience of God, however it comes to you. Remember that Christianity is not a notion but a way.

#4: Do you try to set aside times of quiet for openness to the Holy Spirit? All of us need to find a way into silence which allows us to deepen our awareness of the divine and to find the inward source of our strength. Seek to know an inward stillness, even amid the activities of daily life. Do you encourage in yourself and in others a habit of dependence on God's guidance for each day? Hold yourself and others in the Light, knowing that all are cherished by God.

#7: Be aware of the spirit of God at work in the ordinary activities and experience of your daily life. Spiritual learning continues throughout life, and often in unexpected ways. There is inspiration to be found all around us, in the natural world, in the sciences and arts, in our work and friendships, in our sorrows as well as in our joys. Are you open to new light, from whatever source it may come? Do you approach new ideas with discernment?

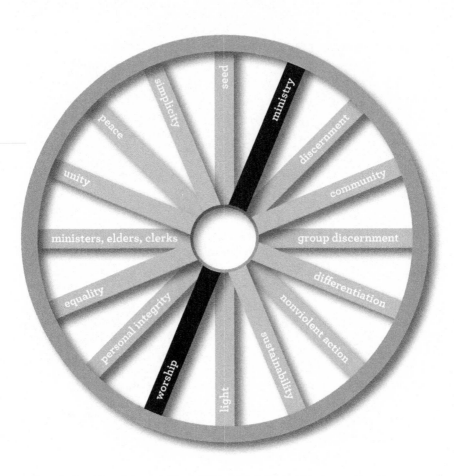

CHAPTER 2

A Prophetic People

We do not live a sustainable life alone. We are sustained by relationships that nourish our spirits and by communities that both encourage us and challenge us to live more faithfully into the measure of light we have been given. The seed that is growing to new life in us is not only a new self. George Fox wrote, "the seed is one, even if ye be ten thousand." Life in the seed unites us with God, with one another, and with all creation. So the Quaker practices of personal spiritual formation that we explored in the preceding chapter in terms of light and seed lead on to the communal spiritual practices of worship and ministry. The mysterious interaction of silence and speaking is the dynamic we now contemplate.

Worship in silence is the most striking feature of Quaker faith and practice for many newcomers to Friends. Meeting for worship is swept bare of liturgical arrangements. There are historical reasons for this. Friends emerged at the end of the English Reformation. Their worship was in many ways the logical conclusion of a process that increasingly pared away the accumulated liturgical and sacramental rites of medieval Catholicism. After the Reformation had reduced the seven sacraments of Catholicism to two, Quakers further insisted that even communion and baptism are best experienced inwardly. The symbolic, ritual use of outward "elements" — water, bread and wine — can lead one away from the reality of communion and baptism as easily as they lead toward it. True communion with God and one another takes place at the center of our beings, as we yield to the light within. Likewise, we are truly baptized as many times as we surrender ourselves and enter the living stream. Furthermore, true vocal ministry and prayer take place by the direct leading of the Spirit. Outward sacraments symbolize the mystery of faith. Quaker worship aims to *experience* the mystery from the inside.

George Fox and early Friends didn't claim to have invented silent worship. We know that some informal groups of English Seekers were already gathering in silent worship before they encountered Friends. Charles Marshall was a teenaged participant in such a group in Bristol in the early 1650s.

> *And in those times . . . there were many who were seeking after the Lord, and there were a few of us who kept one day a week in fasting and prayer. . . . We sat down sometimes in silence; and as any found a concern on their spirits, and inclination in their hearts, they kneeled down and sought the Lord; so that sometimes, before the day ended, there might be twenty of us pray, men and women, and on some of these occasions children spake a few words in prayer; and we were sometimes greatly bowed and broken before the Lord in humility and tenderness.*[1]

Seekers began to worship in silence because they could no longer believe in the liturgical forms of Christian worship. They waited in silence for something new to be revealed. But after hearing the Quaker message, they felt the same silence infused by a powerful new energy. When they learned how to "stand still in the light," to "sink down to the seed," Seekers no longer felt lost. They had been *found*. Francis Howgill described the transformation of Westmoreland Seekers in 1652:

> *The Lord of Heaven and earth we found to be near at hand, and, as we waited upon him in pure silence, our minds out of all things, his heavenly presence appeared in our assemblies, when there was no language, tongue or speech from any creature. The Kingdom of Heaven did gather us and catch us all, as in a net. . . . We came to know a place to stand in and what to wait in; and the Lord appeared daily to us, to our astonishment, amazement and great admiration, insomuch that we often said to one unto another with great joy of heart: "What, is the Kingdom of God come to be with men?" . . . And from that day forward, our hearts were knit unto the Lord and one*

unto another in true and fervent love, in the covenant of Life with God.[2]

No longer waiting *for* God to intervene in their lives, Seekers turned Quakers waited *upon* the Lord in surrender of their own wills, "our minds out of all things." As we heard it described in various ways by Quaker writers in the previous chapter, they found "a place to stand in and what to wait in." They felt in their own bodies the prophecy of Isaiah (40:28-31) fulfilled:

Have you not known? Have you not heard? The Lord is the everlasting God, the Creator of the ends of the earth. He does not faint or grow weary; his understanding is unsearchable. He gives power to the faint, and strengthens the powerless. Even youths will faint and be weary, and the young will fall exhausted; but those who wait upon the Lord shall renew their strength, they shall mount up with wings like eagles, they shall run and not be weary, they shall walk and not faint.

Here is a sustainable life. These "panting souls" (as we heard Penington call Seekers in the preceding chapter) became tireless, incandescent witnesses to the living God, powered by no less than the creator of heaven and earth.

A Prophetic Spirituality

What is it to "wait upon the Lord"? It is to put one's entire being at the disposal of the divine mind and will. It is a readiness to be God's witness in word and action. These traits mark Quaker worship as a *prophetic* spirituality. Today we often think of the "prophet" as someone who speaks out on difficult or controversial social issues, and who is prepared to face incomprehension, rejection, or worse for the message. There have been many such prophets in Quaker history. But more basically, in the biblical tradition, the prophet is someone who develops a deep listening relationship with God, who waits to be called to service, and who speaks or acts out a message received from the divine. That is the essence of Quaker worship and ministry. We wait in silence upon the one who can teach us directly in our hearts. Mostly, that teaching is at a level beyond thoughts and words. We commune with the deeply healing presence of God, who transforms us in subtle but profound ways beyond our awareness. But occasionally, we are given a specific message. It may be just for ourselves to absorb, perhaps to act upon in our lives. Or it may be a message meant for the group in worship at that moment. In that case it is a call to rise and speak.

In the past century, many have preferred to call Quaker spirituality *mystical*. Rufus Jones defined mysticism simply as faith that is grounded in experience. By such a definition, we may call Quakerism mystical. But then Jones added that it's group mysticism, because it is not just about individual experience. Then he further added that Quakerism is prophetic and moral, because it has a social dimension, a concern for justice and peace.[3] Well, when a term has to be qualified in several ways like that, it's often not the most apt term in the first place. But when we compare Quaker faith and practice to the message and method of the prophets and apostles of Hebrew and Christian scriptures, the term *prophetic* integrates all the features Jones felt necessary to add to "mystical."

An anecdote from Fox's *Journal* makes this point. Fox met with some local priests in Margaret Fell's home, Swarthmore Hall, in 1652. In the course of the conversation, "one of them burst out into a passion and said he could speak his experiences as well as I; but I told him experience was one thing but to go with a message and a word from the Lord as the prophets and the apostles had and did, and as I had done to them, this was another thing."[4] *The aim of Quaker worship is that our words and lives speak divine truth and love.*

In more recent decades, some have preferred to equate Quaker worship with *meditation*. Like mysticism, meditation has some overlap with Quaker worship, and a number of Friends have found eastern and western techniques of meditation helpful in centering their attention. Meditation techniques are basically ways of managing the mind, and the human psyche has universal tendencies that can be addressed by meditative traditions both ancient and modern, from both the East and the West. But in the final analysis, Quaker worship is *worship*, not meditation. It is less a goal-oriented activity focused on the self than a way of being in the divine Presence. And the individual's experience of the Presence takes its place within the context of the group's experience. Finally, the readiness to be an instrument of God's communication to the group in spoken ministry lies beyond the realm of meditation. Again, the term *prophetic* is most adequate to Quaker worship and ministry.

Early Friends insisted that they were animated by "the same spirit and power the prophets and apostles were in." That claim scandalized their Puritan contemporaries, who insisted that the prophets and apostles had an extraordinary level of inspiration no longer available. The claim is still scandalous today, for different reasons. It suggests that Quaker faith and practice find greatest coherence within a biblical-Christian frame of reference. It implies that Friends participate in a spiritual life that is not just for their own benefit but that contributes to a vast process of divine purpose in history. The deep structures of Quaker faith and practice may be found in the stories and testimony of the biblical prophets and apostles.

Most centrally, Quaker faith and practice are formed by a deep reflection on the gospel accounts of the life and death of Jesus of Nazareth and by a deep immersion in the Spirit of the living Christ. Quaker practice and vocabulary are most coherent from that perspective. Certainly, "light" and "seed" can be useful images for describing Quaker spiritual experience without reference to the biblical framework where Friends derived them. But within that framework, they speak with far greater resonance. They reveal that our personal spiritual struggle participates in a larger, cosmic drama of liberation and renewal. By "framework" I mean the overall shape, the *gestalt*, of scripture more than particular doctrines or dogmas. In historic Quaker experience, "light" and "seed" are ways we experience the living Christ within and among us. At the same time, as we read scripture, we learn more explicitly who that person is and what kind of life he led — and leads.

The prophetic faith is grounded in a sense of peoplehood. The prophet stands and speaks among his or her people. The First Letter of Peter 2:9 addresses the early Christian community as "a chosen race, a royal priesthood, a holy nation, a people for God's possession, in order that you may proclaim the mighty acts of him who called you out of darkness into his marvelous light." To be a chosen people of God is not an elite status. It is a calling to a particular service to God, to articulate and to demonstrate as a community through time what an individual cannot. It is surely with irony that the writer addresses early Christians as "a chosen race." They were gathered together from all kinds of people around the Eastern Mediterranean. They were a "race" in that they had been powerfully transformed, even reborn, by answering the call "out of darkness into his marvelous light." They were "chosen" in that this wide variety of self-possessed individuals had been called together to become "a people for God's possession," witnesses in word and deed to God's goodness.

Likewise, to be drawn into Quaker faith and practice today is to respond at some deep level to a calling into *peoplehood*. Of course, participation in a Friends meeting should satisfy personal needs and desires. But that is not the real goal or meaning of faith and practice. It is the far greater venture of placing one's own gifts, insights, and worth at the disposal of a group, which in turn places itself at the disposal of divine, imponderable purposes in the world. It is the mystery — indeed, the *sacrament* — of finding the best one has to offer individually raised to another level of worth and meaning when submitted to the processes of the community. Worship is literally "worth-ship." Worship places the infinite worth of each individual at the service of the all-transcending worth of God, who reconciles our incommensurable differences into a wisdom of "rich variety" (Eph. 3:10). Thus, each person's unique worthiness finds its greatest worth through the group and its consecration to God.

Again, this is more than "group mysticism." A prophetic people finds its true identity and purpose as part of a "great cloud of witnesses" (Heb. 12:1) extending into the ancient past. Moreover, it lives and moves toward a far horizon: the destiny of the human race and of all God's creation. That destiny is not a triumphalist notion that everyone should become Christian, much less Quaker! A chosen people lives into its unique identity and purpose among other communities, movements, and causes, set in motion by the divine mystery and converging in ways beyond anyone's reckoning.

The horizon of destiny revealed in the last half-century is the urgent need for the human race to find a sustainable balance with the resources and life systems of the earth. But that destiny will not be reached without a just, equitable, and peaceful society among humans. And none of these things will take place without the key, catalytic role of prophetic minorities who enunciate and experimentally prefigure that destiny. And none of them will be empowered to make that witness without a living experience of that destiny here and now. The apocalyptic revelation of God – the future breaking into the present – bestows that gift.

Apocalyptic? We often think of "apocalypse" as the bizarre, cataclysmic end of the world that fundamentalist Christians believe in and make predictions about. But the basic meaning of the Greek word *apokalypsis* is "revelation," taking the veil off present things, dis-covering their deeper reality and ultimate destiny. The light reveals the true nature of our lives and draws us into the destiny of blessing that God intends for us and all creation. Apocalypse is not about predictions; it's about an experience that profoundly alters our very being. And as communities experience and enact it together, it's the end of a world and the beginning of a new one.

George Fox addressed that experience in his first published tract, *To All That Would Know the Way to the Kingdom* (1653). The *shalom* of God – the integrative peace of social justice and harmony with creation – is known first by waiting upon the Lord, by "standing still in the light":

> The first step of peace is to stand still in the light (which dis-covers things contrary to it) for power and strength to stand against that nature which the light discovers: for here grace grows, here is God alone glorified and exalted, and the unknown truth, unknown to the world, made manifest, which draws up that which lies in prison and refresheth it in time, up to God, out of time, through time.[5]

In personal spiritual practice, and even more in the meeting for worship, we discover "the Way to the Kingdom." Or in Gandhi's words, we begin living the world we want to see. Centering in the light's loving gaze, however, we also discover ways in which we are living contrarily to that reality we most dearly desire. But here we also find the strength to resist the force of these alienated habits.

Along the way a hidden life (the seed of new being) gradually emerges. In silent Quaker worship there is a mysterious interplay of time and eternity ("in time, up to God, out of time, through time"). Our destiny, the destiny of all creation, becomes present here and now, transforming us together. As we shall find in succeeding chapters, that transformation has been intimated in various poetic ways by the ancient Hebrew prophets, who faithfully waited upon the Lord in their own time and place.

The Way into Meeting for Worship

Quaker worship and ministry are a bold venture. How do we enter that amazing reality? William Taber describes it as entering through a series of "doors," into a deep communion.

> When we have once entered into that experience of communion, we realize that we did not create it through our action of worship; all we did was to enter a reality which has always been there from the beginning of time, waiting for us to join it, for "In the beginning was the Word." Devout souls across history have experienced this reality, this Logos. It is always here within us and beside us, available to us as an invisible stream into which we can step at any time. The heart of worship is communion with this invisible but eternal stream of reality in which is the living and eternal Christ.[6]

Taber stresses the importance of regular spiritual devotion, "the door before," which prepares us for meeting for worship. The individual's "daily retirement of mind" enriches not only his or her personal experience but the quality of group worship: "when even just a few meeting attenders have regularly gone through the Door Before, the entire meeting tends to settle more easily into the deep and living quiet which Friends have called a 'gathered' meeting."[7] Taber recommends some practices that help us enter the door before. These include deepening one's appreciation of beauty in its many forms, including nature, the arts, "the faces and graces of people," and even environments we usually find ugly.

The meeting for worship really begins before the stated time. Often the most "gathered" meeting experiences have been engendered by some members upholding the meeting in prayer earlier in the morning, perhaps even the evening before or at times during the week. But it doesn't necessarily come easily. The experienced Friend as well as the new attender struggles at times to enter "the door inward." Taber offers various exercises that can help one "center down," enter the divine communion of worship. "The first and most important approach is to remember that you are always *already* in the Presence."[8] He suggests such practices as mantras, visualization, and prayers. But he cautions,

> All these suggestions make it sound as if we are doing some-
> thing, as if it all depends on us. While a few of these techniques
> may be helpful to some people, especially in their early years
> of attending Quaker meetings, most people eventually come
> to realize that as we learn to relax our anxiety to do the right
> thing, and as we learn what it feels like just to be present, then
> technique becomes far less important than our desire to be
> fully present.[9]

Silence, the absence of words, is only the most superficial impression of this movement into presence. There is a quieting of the restless mind and the moody heart, before one comes to the *still center* that knows the presence. In counseling a distressed and distracted seeker in 1658, George Fox wrote,

> Be still and cool in thy own mind and spirit from thy own
> thoughts, and then thou wilt feel the principle of God to turn
> thy mind to the Lord God, whereby thou wilt receive his
> strength and power from whence life comes, to allay all tem-
> pests. . . . That is it which moulds up into patience, into
> innocency, into soberness, into stillness, into stayedness, into
> quietness, up to God, with his power. When you are in trans-
> gression of the life of God in the particular [i.e., in yourself],
> the mind flies up in the air, and the creature is led into the
> night, and nature goes out of his course. . . . Therefore be still
> a while from thy own thoughts, searching, seeking, desires
> and imaginations, and be stayed in the principle of God in
> thee . . . and thou wilt find strength from him and find him to
> be a present help in time of trouble.[10]

That still center is where we truly meet, with one another and with the eternal One.

Hopefully, worshipers begin to feel a settling, a gathering, a "covering" by the Spirit. Each participant's personal practice is taken hold of by a larger reality. Taber calls this entering the door within, or "the mind of Christ," where "our analytical mind is now a tool rather than a master, as if it has become cushioned in a vaster mind with access to wider ways of knowing." This can be a sublime sense of "inward healing, accompanied with joy, peace, praise for the wonders of creation, or even a comforting sense of great inner space and emptiness before God." But "we need not be surprised if, in the midst of the peace of a gathered meeting, we find ourselves confronting some unpleasant situation in our lives, or we become aware of something about ourselves that troubles or pains us."[11] The divine presence is a healing power. But healing into wholeness also includes identifying and letting go of what is out of place and holds us back.

Thomas Kelly's essay, "The Gathered Meeting," gives rich, poetic expression to the experience of many Friends:

> In the practice of group worship on the basis of silence come special times when the electric hush and solemnity and depth of power steals over the worshipers. A blanket of divine covering comes over the room, a stillness that can be felt is over all, and the worshipers are gathered into a unity and synthesis of life which is amazing indeed. A quickening Presence pervades us, breaking down some part of the special privacy and isolation of our individual lives and blending our spirits within a super-individual Life and Power. An objective, dynamic Presence enfolds us all, nourishes our souls, speaks glad, unutterable comfort within us, and quickens us in depths that had before been slumbering. The Burning Bush has been kindled in our midst, and we stand together on holy ground.[12]

Vocal ministry, a prophetic word, may arise from this place. But it also leads the group more fully *to* this same place. Thus, worship and ministry, silence and speaking, inform and deepen one another. A message in meeting may inspire other messages to be spoken.

But one should beware of speaking too soon. Let the message have time to settle in with the group. Also, avoid "answering" another Friend's ministry, either to agree or to counter it.

The apostle Paul (1 Cor. 14:29-32) describes something similar in early Christian worship:

> *Let two or three prophets speak, and let the others weigh what is said. If a revelation is made to someone else sitting nearby, let the first person be silent. For you can all prophesy one by one, so that all may learn and all be encouraged. And the spirits of the prophets are subject to the prophets, for God is not a God of disorder but of peace.*

In his commentary on this text, Clarence Tucker Craig suggests,

> *The service resembled the Quaker form more nearly than any in existence today, not because of any stress upon silence, but because every member was free to speak as he was moved by the Spirit. There was only one restriction: everything was to be done for mutual edification and nothing as private exhibitionism.*[13]

But the quality of speaking Craig identifies here is produced by the quality of the silence that Paul enjoins upon the group.

Kelly emphasizes the transforming power of prayer in worship:

> *Vocal prayer, poured out from a humble heart, frequently shifts a meeting from a heady level of discussion to the deeps of worship. Such prayers serve as an unintended rebuke to our shallowness and drive us deeper into worship, and commitment. They open the gates of devotion, adoration, submission, confession. They help to unite the group at the level at which real unity is sought. For unity in the springs of life's motivations is far more significant than unity in phrases or outward manners. Such prayers not only "create" that unity; they also give voice to it, and the worshipers are united in a silent amen of gratitude.*[14]

Regrettably, vocal prayer has become rare in most meetings today. But speaking *to* God, the One in whose eternal wisdom we are united, may serve the group better than our speculations *about* God — especially when our Friend is with us in the room! Early in his life, in 1914, the Jewish religious philosopher Martin Buber was asked if he believed in God. He responded, "If to believe in God means to be able to speak about Him in the third person, I do not believe in God. . . . But if to believe in God means to say 'Thou' to Him, then I do."

Vocal Ministry

There is no formula for knowing certainly if one is being led to rise and speak in the meeting for worship. But a Spirit-led message is more than an intriguing idea, a passionate feeling, or a personal story — although it may include any of these. It comes from a deeper place, from the still center in our bodies, and from the body of Friends who are meeting for worship. It may be useful to chart the coordinates of that still center where ministry comes from. It may be schematized as the intersection of four key paradoxes:

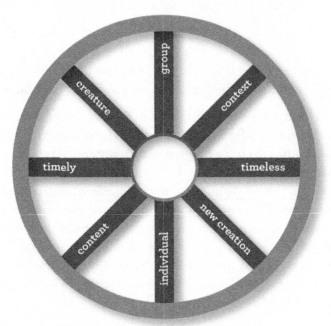

Let us explore these paradoxes one by one.

Individual and Group

When the group enters "the mind of Christ," personal conscious-ness participates in a larger reality. A leading to minister will be shaped by that larger reality. The message is individual in that it is grounded in personal experience and finds expression through a person's own thoughts and words. But it is shaped, both through and beyond the speaker's intention, by the life and needs of the group in that moment. It may also speak to larger concerns in the world, but should not lapse into political rhetoric and speculation. The speaker should beware that his or her thoughts may be framed and prefab-ricated by the media: for example, an interesting story or disturbing report heard on public radio that morning. The person feeling moved to speak should ask whether this message engages with the life and concerns of this meeting. Such queries and prayerful test-ing should precede rising to speak. But as Lewis Benson observes,

> *Ministry is never good or bad in itself. It is not an end in itself. It is for the sake of those who are gathered in the name of Jesus to wait for a word from their Lord. The effect of a minis-ter's words should be to strengthen the sense of being a people gathered to Christ to serve, witness and suffer in his name. Ministry that has a scattering or disintegrating effect on the congregation is to be looked upon with suspicion.*[15]

Taber recalls that as he developed in ministry,

> *I came to know what I had merely believed before – that my ministry belonged to the meeting, not to me. I discovered that while the effectiveness of my ministry did depend somewhat on my faithfulness, it depended far more than I had realized on the invisible, hidden faithfulness of people who seldom if ever spoke in meeting.*[16]

Similarly, Kelly cherishes his experience of meetings

> *in which no one person, no one speech, stands out as the one that "made" the meeting, those hours wherein the personali-ties that take part verbally are not enhanced as individuals in the eyes of others, but are subdued and softened and lost sight of because, in the language of Fox, "The Lord's Power*

was over all." Brevity, earnestness, sincerity and frequently a lack of polish characterized the best Quaker speaking.[17]

So there is a paradoxical quality to vocal ministry in the manner of Friends. The message is yours and it is not yours. Ultimately, it is neither the individual nor the group, but the divine Presence that speaks through us.

Content and Context

The individual is led to rise and speak a *specific* message. One should consider it prayerfully before rising. But one should not plan too specifically. The Spirit that is prompting, nudging, even forcing one to stand will also lead, phrase by phrase. Moreover, one should not aim for grammatical precision, oratory polish, or conceptual completeness. Often a brief, even fragmentary message leaves more space for its meaning to be completed by its hearers, according to their own "conditions."

At the same time, the specific content develops in relation to its context. The prophetic word is a word for a specific person to speak to a specific group at a specific moment, not another. For this reason, a message that feels vital for one meeting for worship must not be saved for a later one, or spoken to another group without a specific, renewed leading. It is like the manna the Israelites collected each morning in the wilderness. It is the bread of life for this group today. If it is saved for another day, it spoils and may even be harmful.

But again like manna (which means literally, "what's this?"), the speaker does not fully understand the message or why it is to be given here and now. Of course, he or she has ideas and intentions. But anyone who has participated in a conversation after meeting about a message realizes that people derive very different things from it. Still deeper meanings may be hidden from everyone, but mysteriously draw those participating into a greater wisdom.

Timely and Timeless

The prophetic word is ephemeral in the sense of its unique configuration of content and context. In the larger sense, however, our human condition and circumstances are the ephemeral element.

The divine word is eternal, but emerges in specific ways to the endlessly shifting dynamics of our personal and group existence, not to mention the passing of entire generations. Isaiah (40:6, 8) witnesses, "A voice says, 'Cry out!' And I said, 'What shall I cry?' All people are grass, their constancy is like the flower of the field. . . . The grass withers, the flower fades; but the word of our God will stand forever."

The prophetic word is both timeless and timely. The prophet is possessed by an urgent leading. Yet in another sense, the prophet has *more* than all the time in the world. The prophet neither counsels complacency nor seeks to stampede others into action. The prophet is neither a progressive, with rosy predictions for the future, nor a reactionary, looking longingly backward, frightened of change. The prophetic word is an insight into the *present*. George Fox wrote in 1652, "Oh! Be faithful! Look not back, nor be too forward, further than ye have attained; for ye have no time, but this present time: therefore prize your time for your souls' sake. And so, grow up in that which is pure, and keep to the oneness."[18]

It is true that Quaker prophetic ministry has consistently augured for social progress. Quaker ministry has been the work of both women and men, rich and poor. Arising from their experience of prophetic worship and ministry, Friends became standard bearers for more equal relations between women and men, religious freedom, the abolition of slavery, racial justice, civil rights, prison reform, and more. They made these contributions not through great visions for the future, but through deep insight and stubborn faithfulness in the present. Early and traditional Friends appear at least as much like conservatives as they do progressives. But they were neither. They advocated for a more just and peaceful society. But most of all, they stood still in the light, day by day, spoke truth from that place, and let the powers make their decisions in response. And some things changed.

Standing still in the light, sinking down to the seed, is at times a deep immersion in suffering. It requires patience with ourselves — the same patience God has practiced in abiding with us all along. But it is also an impetus to change, to grow, to live more fully day by day into the wisdom, power and goodness of the light. Both patience and impetus are integral to the covenant of light. Prophetic ministry in the meeting for worship certainly requires patience toward a group bound up with various inertias. But it is also a loving announcement of "the day of the Lord," a call for greater self-knowledge and change.

Living more fully in the light may also lead individuals and meetings to take actions to renounce cherished luxuries or to confront social mores or civil authority. These prophetic steps involve suffering, slight or serious. Friends have traditionally called this movement "taking up the cross." It begins with patient waiting upon the Lord in worship, which itself is not always easy. It continues with faithfully speaking in vocal ministry, whether others receive it happily or not. And it leads on to prophetic action in our lives and our communities, which may encounter resistance and hostility. But one important effect of our suffering is that it "enlarges the borders of the heart" to the suffering of others. Like the cross of Jesus, it "sheds love abroad to the world."

Often in Friends meetings, we hear heartfelt pangs expressed for the suffering of friends and neighbors, for people of other lands and races, for other species of life on the earth. Implicitly or explicitly, these cries are prayers for God's help, for justice and the end of violence. Here we find ourselves in the place of Job (19:23-27), who, immersed in his own unaccountable suffering, insists upon the redeeming justice of God.

> O that my words were written down! O that they were inscribed in a book! O that with an iron pen and with lead they were engraved on a rock forever! For I know that my Redeemer lives, and that at last he will stand upon the earth; and after my skin has been thus destroyed, then in the flesh I shall see God, whom I shall see on my side, and my eyes shall behold, and not another. My heart faints within me!

Job's pained, angry urgency is matched by his timeless conviction of God's justice and mercy.

Writing to Friends in the ministry in 1654, George Fox cautioned, "Friends, be not hasty; for he that believes in the Light makes not haste. . . . In that [Light] wait to receive power, and the

Lord God almighty preserve you. Whereby you may come to feel the Light which comprehends time and the world and fathoms it."[19]

Creature and New Creation

In the ongoing life of a particular Friends meeting, we hear certain familiar themes and concerns (perhaps even "hobby horses") from particular Friends. We may recognize them in ourselves as well. The old Quaker expression, "the water tastes of the pipes," acknowledges that even the most inspired message is marked by the personality of the speaker. Vocal ministry emerges from the paradox that we are both creatures with natural abilities, limitations, wounds, hopes, and sorrows *and* an emerging new creation with spiritual gifts, divine calling, and destiny. Living as closely as we can in the middle of that paradox, we learn to speak compassionately, but with a discernment that does not gloss over human self-deceptions and prejudices.

From that paradoxical place, we learn to recognize the leading to speak from certain physical, creaturely symptoms, like a quickening pulse or even quaking. Lewis Benson observes that these signs may induce "feelings of weakness and inadequacy . . . [but] if the call is really from God strength will be given."[20] Even experienced public speakers and preachers may (and should) feel awe, even dread, of speaking out of the silence. It is a weighty thing.

In the Gospel of John, when Jesus first calls his disciples together, he promises them, "you will see heaven opened and the angels [literally, "messengers"] of God ascending and descending upon the Son of Man" (John 1:51). At first, they probably thought it would come as a mystical vision. But over time, they realized that *they were the vision*, they were the messengers as they spoke in the Spirit of Jesus (the Son of Man). We too become messengers as we become receptive to the word of life. To speak in meeting for worship is to serve as a messenger between heaven and earth. We communicate earth to heaven when we "hold one another in the light," when we pray on behalf of the meeting and all creatures who suffer. Conversely, we communicate heaven to earth as we speak words of compassion, hope, and prophetic challenge, in whatever idiom, Christian or other, we are gifted to use.

For 350 years and over many generations, Friends have learned how to co-create the mystery of Quaker worship and ministry. Caroline Stephen witnessed in 1908, "in the united stillness of a truly gathered meeting there is a power known only by experience, and mysterious even when most familiar."[21] Many have shared the experience of Mary Penington who like her husband, Isaac, had long searched for a worship that felt authentic:

> Oh! The joy that filled my soul in the first meeting ever held in our house at Chalfont. To this day I have a fresh remembrance of it. It was then the Lord enabled me to worship him in that which was undoubtedly his own, and give up my whole strength, yea, to swim in the life which overcame me that day ... for I could say, "This is it which I have longed and waited for, and feared I never should have experienced."[22]

But it is important to acknowledge that not every meeting for worship experiences "gathering" in the Spirit. Kelly speaks to that fact:

> Like the individual soul, the group must learn to endure spiritual weather without dismay. Some hours of worship are full of glow and life, but others lack the quality. The disciplined soul, and the disciplined group, have learned to cling to the reality of God's presence, whether the feeling of presence is great or faint. If only the group has been knit about the very springs of motivation, the fountain of the will, then real worship has taken place. . . . If no blanket of divine covering is warmly felt, and if the wills have been offered together in the silent work of worship, worshipers may go home content and nourished, and say, "It was a good meeting." In the venture of group worship, souls must learn to accept spiritual "weather" and go deeper, in will, into Him who makes all things beautiful in their time.[23]

The urgent search for a sustainable life is no less urgent a search for deeper grounding in our personal lives and our group practices of worship and ministry. The challenges are simply too overwhelming if we do not draw consistently upon the wellsprings of life within and among us. The prophetic worship and ministry described here in turn ground the social testimonies and discernment processes of Friends, as we shall see in the following chapters.

Advices and Queries from Britain Yearly Meeting's *Quaker Faith & Practice*

#9: In worship we enter with reverence into communion with God and respond to the promptings of the Holy Spirit. Come to meeting for worship with heart and mind prepared. Yield yourself and all your outward concerns to God's guidance so that you may find "the evil weakening in you and the good raised up."

#12: When you are preoccupied and distracted in meeting let wayward and disturbing thoughts give way quietly to your awareness of God's presence among us and in the world. Receive the vocal ministry of others in a tender and creative spirit. Reach for the meaning deep within it, recognizing that even if it is not God's word for you, it may be so for others. Remember that we all share responsibility for the meeting for worship whether our ministry is in silence or through the spoken word.

#13: Do not assume that vocal ministry is never to be your part. Faithfulness and sincerity in speaking, even very briefly, may open the way to fuller ministry from others. When prompted to speak, wait patiently to know that the leading and the time are right, but do not let a sense of your own unworthiness hold you back. Pray that your ministry may arise from deep experience, and trust that words will be given to you. Try to speak audibly and distinctly, and with sensitivity to the needs of others. Beware of speaking predictably or too often, and of making additions towards the end of a meeting when it was well left before.

CHAPTER 3

"Mind the Oneness"

In the preceding chapter, we read George Fox's teaching that "The first step of peace is to stand still in the light." He explains that the light discloses those things that are "contrary" to itself, while giving us the power and strength to live and act with grace. The light brings into focus habits in our lives that are addictive, excessive, or just unhelpful. It causes us to question how much we need to consume and to possess. In some cases, we become aware of things that are morally wrong, sinful. But more often, we realize that we just don't need to have or do some things. They are cluttering our schedules, our homes, our consciences. We need to let them go if we are to live more fully and transparently in the light. And, as Fox adds, the light gives us the strength to shed them.

A sustainable life is streamlined to "go the distance" of a day, a week, a year, a lifetime. That means that we add new possessions, activities, even beliefs with thoughtful care, asking what really fits the whole. Those questions are a matter of discernment; we require meditative reflection and prayerful search for God's will in the decisions that shape our lives, from major vocational questions to choices of how to furnish and maintain our homes. Discernment helps us grow in integrity. And as we grow in integrity, become more whole persons, our discernment grows sharper and takes us further. This chapter focuses on that crucial interaction.

Personal integrity is about living an integral life, integrating what is vital into a coherent whole, and releasing the rest. It is to be *consistent*, the same in life as we are in words, not promising more than we can accomplish, not conforming to popular opinions we don't really believe, not acquiring habits that are unhealthy and that don't contribute to a just and peaceful world. Living with integrity is to *resist* violating our own consciences in order to fit in with the crowd or to please someone important. Integrity is *wholeness*. To live an integral life is to "mind the oneness," as Fox urges. Early Quakers called themselves "Friends of Truth." The Hebrew word for truth, *amun*, literally means "solid," "consistent." To befriend the truth is to become consistent in word and deed with the truth we receive from the light in our consciences. Truth is more fundamentally participational than propositional. We live into the truth most of all through our actions.

So integrity comes in part through *renunciation*. The tradition of Quaker integrity began with three key resistances by early Friends. First, they refused to recite creeds. They saw how doctrinal conformity had produced a culture of hypocrisy in Puritan England. People mouthed tenets they either didn't understand or didn't believe. They avowed moral standards they didn't keep. Friends didn't reject Christian belief, but they pressed the question we heard from Fox in Chapter 1: "You will say, Christ saith this, and the apostles say this, but what canst thou say? Art thou a child of the light, and hast thou walked in the light, and what thou speakest, is it inwardly from God?"

Second, they refused to swear oaths. Living through the English Civil War and several changes in government in just a few years, they had seen people swear oaths of allegiance to one government and then another, regimes diametrically opposed to each other. Oaths were another invitation to hypocrisy and deceit. Friends promised to live peacefully under any government, and to be legally accountable to that promise. But their refusal to swear oaths made them suspicious to civil authorities. Many were imprisoned for their refusal to swear.

Finally, contrary to standard commercial practice, Friends refused to bargain, either as sellers or buyers. As merchants, they set what they believed was a fair price and let customers decide for or against. Their practice began to establish the Quaker reputation for integrity in business and placed Friends on the forefront of England's commercial revolution. The call to integrity is challenging. Fox's counsel in Chapter 1 rings true: "earthly reason will tell you what ye shall lose. Hearken not to that, but stand still in the Light ... and then strength comes from the Lord, and help, contrary to your expectation." Thus, integrity had religious, political, and economic dimensions for early Friends.

The Quaker sense of integrity was inspired in part by the Sermon on the Mount. There Jesus comments, "You have heard . . . 'You shall not swear falsely, but carry out the vows you have made to the Lord.' But I say to you, Do not swear at all. . . . Let your word be 'Yes, Yes' or 'No, No.' Anything more than this comes from evil" (Mat. 5:33–37). Jesus stresses a *singleness* of vision and devotion: "The eye is the lamp of the body. So, if your eye is healthy ["single" in the King James Version] your whole body will be full of light, but if your eye is unhealthy, your whole body will be full of darkness. . . . No one can serve two masters, for a slave will either hate the one and love the other, or be devoted to the one and despise the other. You cannot serve God and wealth" (6:22-24).

Against religious hypocrisy, Jesus warns, "Not everyone who says to me, 'Lord, Lord,' will enter the kingdom of heaven, but only the one who does the will of my Father in heaven" (7:21). Against material worries and wants, he counsels purity of heart: "Therefore do not worry, saying, 'What will we eat?' or 'What will we drink?' or 'What will we wear?' For . . . your heavenly Father knows that you need all these things. But strive first for the kingdom of God and his righteousness, and all these things will be given to you as well" (6:31-33).

Integrity includes even the love of enemies: "I say to you, Love your enemies and pray for those who persecute you, so that you may be children of your Father in heaven, for he makes the sun rise on the evil and on the good, and sends rain on the righteous and on the unrighteous. For if you love those who love you, what reward do you have? . . . Be perfect, therefore, as your heavenly Father is perfect" (5:44-48). The Greek word here for "perfect" is *teleios*: "complete," "mature," "whole." Perfection is integrity, a mature oneness that draws even enemies to its heart, refusing to let antagonisms and dualisms have the last word.

Testimony

So we can hear not only integrity but simplicity, equality, and peacemaking implied in the Sermon on the Mount. According to

Wilmer Cooper, "integrity" provides the most adequate one-word definition of Quaker faith and practice. It is "the essential Quaker testimony and undergirds all the other testimonies of Friends."[1]

The concept of *testimony* is central to Quaker faith and practice. George Fox emphasized that our lives must preach.[2] Our lives communicate what we really believe, whatever our words may profess. Our lives testify whether we really trust God to help us do the right thing. Early and traditional Friends did not speak of various "testimonies" but simply of testimony, a single, undivided, whole life. For example, John Conran, a nineteenth-century Irish Quaker minister, records his struggle in early adulthood to give up fashionable clothing for plain Quaker attire. Finally, "I felt a solemn covering come over my spirit early one morning . . . to conform to the simple appearance of Christ's followers; His garment was all of a piece [John 19:23], so ought mine to be, of a piece with my speech, my life and conversation."[3]

Friends today often speak of "the Quaker testimonies," typically enumerated as simplicity, peace, integrity, community, equality and stewardship (or sustainable living). Together they form a helpful mnemonic, SPICES. While our traditional Quaker commitments may be helpfully categorized in this way, it is important to remember the integral whole they form. Since testimony is the visible practice of an inwardly received truth, it has a sacramental quality for Friends. Testimony is the outward sign of an inward grace. Along these lines, John Punshon writes,

> Inwardly, [the testimonies] are our guide to the nature of our Creator, the source of our inspiration, the medium of our understanding, the particular mystical path of Quakerism, our way to God. Externally, they are our guide to life, a sign of divine love for creation, the means of our prophetic witness. They therefore take their meaning from the highest reality we know.[4]

So the outward practices that form our testimony not only express our inner conviction. They also add further clarity to that conviction. The inward and outward continue to inform and advance one another as we "live up to the light" we have been given. Succeeding chapters will highlight different Quaker testimonies in relation to individual and group practices of spiritual discernment. *One of the aims of this book is to show that the testimonies – indeed all of Quaker faith and practice – are not simply lists of things but form an integral, mutually informing and balancing whole, an undivided, sustainable life.*

Let us briefly return to a theme from this book's Introduction – that we are created in both the image of God and the image of the universe. In the image of God we are endowed with the divine Spirit (see Gen. 2:7). But the Spirit should not be conceived as a separate dimension of our being. God's Spirit (or light, or seed), if we are attentive to it, works to the integration, fulfillment, and redemption of our material lives. It is the second birth that fulfills our first, natural birth. Recalling Paul's words in Romans 8 (again see the Introduction), the Spirit groans in us, in solidarity with the whole creation. It works in us to redeem us from futility, vanity, and entropy. As it orders our lives, it works through us to order the creatures around us in God's love and wisdom. In that way, we live into our divine vocation as the tenders of God's garden. "Spirituality" in any serious, lived sense is a movement into integrity.

John Woolman: Integrity and Discernment

John Woolman was a Quaker minister in colonial New Jersey. His *Journal* offers classic examples of the development of testimony in an undivided life. Woolman had concern for the conditions of Native American peoples and African American slaves, peoples who were suffering from rapid colonial expansion and ruthless exploitation by European American settlers. He held the Quaker conviction of the infinite worth of all peoples before God and the divine light in them all. He was especially pained that some members of his own Religious Society of Friends held slaves. His concern developed into a life of prophetic witness through a series of incidents in which he struggled to maintain personal integrity. Let us look at three key episodes.

He writes that in 1742 (at age 22):

My employer, having a Negro woman, sold her and directed me to write a bill of sale, the man being waiting who bought her. The thing was sudden, and though the thoughts of writing an instrument of slavery for one of my fellow creatures felt uneasy, yet I remembered I was hired by the year, that it was my master who directed me to do it, and that it was an elderly man, a member of our Society, who bought her; so through weakness I gave way and wrote it, but at the executing of it, I was so afflicted in my mind that I said before my master and the Friend that I believed slavekeeping to be a practice inconsistent with the Christian religion. This in some degree abated my uneasiness, yet as often as I reflected seriously upon it I thought I should have been clearer if I had desired to be excused from it as a thing against my conscience, for such it was.[5]

Taken by surprise, he deferred to his employer and the elderly Friend, and wrote the bill of sale, but felt and expressed pangs of conscience, even in the act. An act of unfaithfulness to the truth often provides the painful memory that goads us to rise higher.

Trained in the writing of legal documents, Woolman faced this same dilemma a number of times. As he grew in personal integrity, his witness spoke to the consciences of others. In 1756, now aged 36:

A neighbor [suffering from a serious injury] desired me to write his will. I took notes, and amongst other things he told me to which of his children he gave his young Negro: I considered the pain and distress he was in, and knew not how it would end, so I wrote his will, save only that part concerning his slave, and carrying it to his bedside, read it to him, and then told him in a friendly way, that I could not write any instruments by which my fellow-creatures were made slaves, without bringing trouble on my own mind. I let him know that I charged nothing for what I had done, and desired to be excused from doing the other part in the way he proposed. Then we had a serious conference on the subject, and at length, he agreeing to set her free, I finished his will.[6]

Woolman affected a number of slave owners through these personal encounters. He also became a leading voice moving Friends to renounce slaveholding and manumit their slaves. He was by no means the first or only Friend with this concern. But his articulate integrity made him a central figure.

In his travels as a Quaker minister he found a variety of opportunities to "labor" with slaveholding Friends. He let the boundaries of his personal integrity serve as talking points. For example, on a journey in ministry among Friends in Maryland in 1766, he chose to walk instead of ride a horse, "that by so travelling I might have a more lively feeling of the condition of the oppressed slaves, set an example of lowliness before the eyes of their masters."[7] On various occasions, he refused to be served tea in silver cups or to use sugar. Silver and sugar were typically produced by slave labor. On at least one occasion he left money in payment to the slaves who had served him while visiting the home of a slaveholding Friend. Michael Birkel observes that in such exchanges, "his humility and charity have shone forth. These have not hindered the power of his message. On the contrary, they have enhanced it. By his example he has tried to reach the pure witness in others."[8]

Thus, a journey of conscience and integrity began with a misstep, writing the bill of sale for a slave. But it started Woolman on a path that eventually helped lead Friends as a body to renounce slaveholding. And in years to come, many Friends became political advocates for the abolition of slavery, boycotted slave-produced commodities, and participated in the Underground Railroad to abet fugitive slaves.

The conscientious practice of personal integrity may make one seem eccentric to others. Woolman was sometimes viewed as a bit odd even among Friends, who were markedly countercultural in colonial America. But the humility and genuine warmth with which he communicated increased his persuasive power.

Woolman also felt great compassion for the nonhuman creation. "I was early convinced in my mind that . . . as by [God's] breath the flame of life was kindled in all animal and sensitive creatures [Ps. 104:30], to say we love God . . . and at the same time exercise cruelty toward the least creature . . . was a contradiction in itself."[9]

In his 1763 essay, *A Plea for the Poor*, Woolman defines the issue of integrity succinctly:

To conform a little to a wrong way strengthens the hands of such who carry wrong customs to their utmost extent; and the more a person appears to be virtuous and heavenly-minded, the more powerfully does his conformity operate in favour of evil-doers. . . . While [Friends] profess in all cases to live in constant opposition to that which is contrary to universal righteousness . . . what language is sufficient to set for the strength of those obligations we are under to beware lest by our example we lead others wrong?[10]

Integrity and Discernment

Integrity is the product of deep, constant discernment. As we train ourselves to stand still in the light more consistently, our lives become more transparent. And following the light's leadings, our lives become more coherent. But that coherence comes only partly through the light's intimations. We *interpret* where the light is leading us through various frameworks of understanding. That is, the light within becomes our point of reference within a given frame of reference. We understand our "experience" in part through various interpretive models. In the preceding chapter, we saw that early and traditional Friends understood their experience as a prophetic people within a biblical-Christian frame of reference. Today, individual Friends apply various frames of understanding to their Quaker experience — mystical, meditative, prophetic, Buddhist, feminist, neopagan, and others. I have made the case for the biblical-Christian framework as the most adequate to understanding our experience today as a people of God in history. While each of us will be individually inspired and guided by various spiritual and psychological wisdoms, our life together as a body is most helpfully communicated through the prophetic language of the prophets and apostles.

The case of John Woolman illustrates how discernment takes place within frameworks. In the first story, he felt a strong inner hesitation against writing the bill of sale. When speaking to the two men involved, he told them that "I believed slavekeeping to be a practice inconsistent with the Christian religion." His understanding of Christian faith helped him understand and articulate his "gut-feeling" about slavery — despite the fact that many Christians had no scruple against it, and even defended slavery using the Bible. Quaker historian J. William Frost finds that Woolman utilized a variety of frameworks of interpretation.[11] Among Friends, he favored biblical themes. But in his anti-slavery essays for a wider readership, he combined biblical themes with philosophical ideas from the liberal Enlightenment.

In our own circumstances, we discern our unique path of integrity by the leading of the light, within the frames of understanding that seem most consonant with it. Each of us operates by some improvised (and largely unconscious) system of religious traditions, philosophical ideas, moral values, parental messages from our childhood, and the examples of mentors and models whom we have admired. Our experience over time helps us glean the most important of these into a coherent whole. Conversely, the more coherent our beliefs and values are, the more they help us understand our experience and live with greater integrity.

But integrity, like riding a bicycle, comes more easily when we are moving in a particular direction with some momentum. When we follow a calling and live out a vocation of some kind, many questions are more easily answered. Woolman's calling as a minister (nonprofessional, in the Quaker tradition) focused his life. He purposefully reduced his business commitments, which also meant living a more simple life with his family, in order to be more available for ministry among Friends. Some Friends feel "under the weight of a concern" to work on a religious or social issue for a period of time in their lives. Such Friends feel "singled out to act in response to a spiritual compulsion. This we call concern and distinguish it from those things that we are concerned about."[12] In other words, we feel concerned over many things we see and hear in the world. But to act "under a concern," in this sense, is to re-prioritize and reorganize our lives to be of service in a certain way.

When a Friend faces an important decision — a matter of further education, new employment, marriage, or membership the Religious Society of Friends, for example — she or he may choose to undertake a personal discernment process with a "clearness committee." This is a small, informal group or *ad hoc* committee of the meeting, chosen to help the individual or couple seeking clearness (clarity) about the matter to be decided. The final decision rests with the "focus person" seeking clearness. The exercise of talking about the matter to a small group of wise and sympathetic listeners can itself help clarify what needs to be done. But this small group may be of further service in the process by asking questions that may not have been considered before.

In the case of marriage under the care of the meeting or application for membership in the meeting, the clearness committee is typically chosen jointly by the meeting and the individual(s) seeking clearness. The aim is to find a shared clearness among all participants about whether or how to proceed. That is, a proposed marriage under the care of the meeting should feel like a wise and fulfilling decision to the committee members as well as to the couple, if the meeting is to hold the celebration under its care. Similarly, an individual's step from informal attender to formal member should be made with adequate understanding of Quaker faith and practice, and with a willingness to engage faithfully with Friends in the long term. In both marriage and membership, if clearness is reached, the meeting commits itself to nurture the new member or couple in the future. In the case of discerning a calling or concern, the meeting may even contribute to the material needs of the person whose decisions it endorses.

So in Friends practice, personal discernment is often aided by others. Quaker faith and practice is a bold venture in Spirit-led living. A realistic sense of the human condition tells us that anyone can fall prey to self-deception and wishful thinking in making decisions. There may be major implications for our lives and the lives of others. So it is wise to draw upon Friends who may have greater experience in life and in the Quaker way.

Good descriptions of the clearness committee process are available in Quaker literature. In particular, see *Spiritual Discernment* by Patricia Loring and the book of discipline of New England Yearly Meeting.[13] These guides suggest that the committee only ask questions of the focus person seeking clarity. But it may sometimes be appropriate to offer useful information or describe relevant experiences from committee members' own lives, though it must be made clear that these offerings are not prescriptive for the focus person's decision. The committee's purpose is not to offer advice or tell the person what to do, but to help him or her see the matter more fully, uncovering possible blind spots or unconsidered factors. In general, gently posed, open-ended questions are most useful. The tone of the clearness committee session should be prayerfully serious. But that does not exclude the possibility of good-natured laughter or sympathetic tears. Typically, the focus person will not reach a decision in the one to three sessions spent with the clearness committee. The decision usually unfolds later, with further reflection.

Whether contemplating such a decision alone or with a clearness committee, the focal point of personal discernment may be found at the center of four different axes of consideration. These are schematized here:

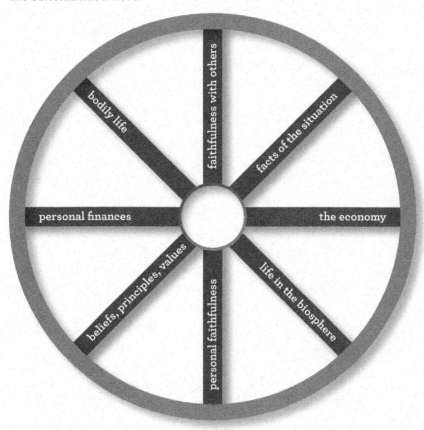

Each axis defines a certain tension or interrelationship within which an important life decision is made. None of them should be discounted as irrelevant, even if some will appear more important than others. Each axis is explored here through some basic queries posed in terms general enough to apply to a wide variety of situations. An individual or clearness committee may wish to adapt and sharpen them to fit the matter at hand.

Personal faithfulness/faithfulness with others

Here story may prove the most useful mode of inquiry. What is the story of your life, and what is the meaning of the matter under discernment in relation to that story? (A long account is probably not necessary, but an important decision will affect some major thread of a person's life.) What is the abiding truth of your life, and how will the proposed action add to it? To whom or what (your understanding of God, or ultimate reality) do you strive to be faithful in your life, and what form has that faithfulness taken? How does the proposed action further your faithfulness?

Meanwhile, with what individuals or communities are you living in faithful relationship? (It might be a partner or spouse, a local Friends meeting, a worship, study, or action group, or a community.) How would this decision affect that relationship? Does it begin a new faithful relationship? Does it end one? Does it redefine a relationship? What is the integrity, or wholeness, of this proposed change?

Beliefs, principles and values/facts of the situation

What vital beliefs, guiding principles, or core values are embodied in the proposed action? Would a decision against this action violate them? Would there be other ways to embody them? Is there any conflict of values, principles, or beliefs implied in this decision? If so, try to define that conflict as clearly as possible.

How do these beliefs, values, and principles engage with the facts of the situation at hand? Is this the right time for the proposed action? Would a later time be better? Or has the opportune moment already passed? Also, is this the right place? Are these the right persons to engage with? Or would another place or other collaborators be more appropriate?

Personal finances/the economy

How does the proposed action affect your personal finances? Would this action be wise in the present economy? Are you sufficiently free of debts and other financial obligations to undertake this new action? Can you fulfill current contracts while undertaking the proposed action? Do you have financial reserves to sustain this action? Will you be able to support financially your local Friends meeting and organizations working to promote justice, peace, and the integrity of creation?

Likewise, how will your financial life and activity under the proposed course of action participate in larger economic institutions and structures? Will it avoid supporting the harsh exploitation or coercion of workers, unequal opportunity in the marketplace, preparations for war, and other blights upon society? If financial investment is involved, will it avoid speculation? Will it empower socially responsible work in the world? Will you invest through socially responsible institutions? (Some may find these questions further afield than others. But it is incumbent on any Friend seeking to live with integrity to consider them.)

Bodily life/life in the biosphere

Will you continue or start healthy habits of eating, exercise, sleep, and other practices to sustain you as you live into the proposed action? Do you recognize these as important factors for your continued life in body, mind, and spirit? Are you aware of these habits as an important influence on the people you will work, study, and live with? Are you committed to the reuse, recycling, and renewal of the materials you use and consume? Are you moderate in your use of fossil fuels? Are you committed to kind treatment and adequate provision for any living beings under your care?

Are you mindful of the impact of your decisions and actions on the earth's biosphere? If you plan to raise children, do you consider their impact upon the planet? While realizing the infinitesimally small increment of difference your decisions will make on the earth's surface, do you sow the seeds of good stewardship and sustainable practices in your tiny niche? To paraphrase Gandhi, are you starting now to live in the world you would like to see?

Taken together, these queries are overwhelming. The aim is not to discourage anyone, but to remind the reader of the scope that the life of integrity must take into discernment, particularly in the modern, relatively affluent society where most readers live. "Right answers" to these queries are not presupposed. Like the traditional advices and queries of Friends, these are intended as questions to live with. We wrestle more acutely with different ones at different moments in our lives. Again, integrity is a lifelong work of self-examination and re-evaluation of choices. Major life-decisions are opportunities to consider a wide variety of changes in personal life, particularly when the proposed action involves a change of work, routine, place of residence, or living arrangements.

———————●———————

We will close with another classic anecdote from John Woolman's *Journal*. In 1761 Woolman met some Native Americans from the Lenni Lenape tribe. "And in conversation with them by an interpreter, as also by observations on their countenance and conduct, I believed some of them were measurably acquainted with that divine power which subjects the rough and froward [sic] will of the creature; and at times I felt inward drawings toward a visit to that place" (i.e., to Wyalusing, about two hundred miles from Philadelphia.[14] As he became clear inwardly and with his wife about making the visit, he laid the matter before his monthly and quarterly meetings, since it was a matter of his ministry under their care. They found unity to support his decision. By the time he made the journey in June 1763, however, war with other tribes made passage to Wyalusing dangerous. Nevertheless, Woolman felt clear to proceed. Bad weather and fear made travel difficult. Along the way, he had time to review once again his leading to make the journey:

> It being a rainy day we continued in our tent, and here I was led
> to think on the nature of the exercise which hath attended me.
> Love was the first motion, and then a concern arose to spend
> some time with the Indians, that I might feel and understand
> their life and the spirit they live in, if haply I might receive some
> instruction from them, or they be in any degree helped forward

by my following the leadings of Truth amongst them. And as it pleased the Lord to make way for my going at a time when the troubles of war were increasing, and when by reason of much wet weather travelling was more difficult than usual at that season, I looked upon it as a more favourable opportunity to season my mind and bring me into a nearer sympathy with them.[15]

So much is distilled in these few sentences. He used idle time in the tent to check his bearings, rather than be simply bored and frustrated with the weather. He traced his motivations, following the leading back to the love he had felt for the Lenni Lenapes he had met. From that "first motion" (initial feeling or motivation) came the concern to spend some time with them. Although he was an esteemed minister among Friends by this time, Woolman saw the trip as an opportunity to learn from the Indians. But he hoped that, if he remained faithful to "the leadings of Truth," he might somehow benefit them as well. Meanwhile, he viewed the danger and discomfort of the journey not as pain and aggravation but as fruitful suffering. *His* discomfort aroused "a nearer sympathy with them" in their difficulties. Through this act of discernment, Woolman found himself refreshed in his relationship with "the great Father of Mercies" and content to continue the journey, notwithstanding the danger and discomfort.

In our own journeys, each of us finds direction and contentment more easily when we stay close to the guide. To all who seek to live whole lives, lives of integrity, Jesus invites, "Come to me, all you that are weary and are carrying heavy burdens, and I will give you rest. Take my yoke upon you, and learn from me; for I am gentle and humble in heart, and you will find rest for your souls. For my yoke is easy, and my burden is light" (Matt. 11:28-30).

Advices and Queries from Britain Yearly Meeting's *Quaker Faith & Practice*

Integrity

#37: Are you honest and truthful in all you say and do? Do you maintain strict integrity in business transactions and in our dealings with individuals and organizations? Do you use money and information entrusted to you with discretion and responsibility? Taking oaths implies a double standard of truth; in choosing to affirm instead, be aware of the claim to integrity you are making.

#38: If pressure is brought upon you to lower your standard of integrity, are you prepared to resist it? Our responsibilities to God and our neighbour may involve us in taking unpopular stands. Do not let the desire to be sociable, or the fear of seeming peculiar, determine your decisions.

Personal Discernment

#27: Live adventurously. When choices arise, do you take the way that offers the fullest opportunity for the use of your gifts in the service of God and the community? Let your life speak. When decisions have to be made, are you ready to join with others in seeking clearness, asking for God's guidance and offering counsel to one another?

#28: Every stage of our lives offers fresh opportunities. Responding to divine guidance, try to discern the right time to undertake or relinquish responsibilities without undue pride or guilt. Attend to what love requires of you, which may not be great busyness.

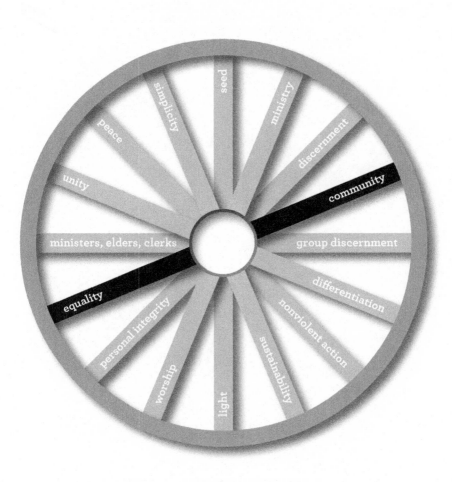

CHAPTER 4

Testimony in Conversation

In an increasingly secular and fragmented society, many today feel a deep yearning for "community," an intimacy of relationship and unity of purpose with others. Meanwhile, in a highly mediated society of global electronic communications, we are distressed by reports of so many kinds of unequal opportunity and uneven access to resources to meet human needs. And precisely because our existence is so compartmentalized today, we often fail to recognize the relationship between these two concerns. Indeed, Friends today tend to think of "equality" and "community" as two different social testimonies, when in reality they are two aspects of our single testimony. And when we recognize that testimony *testifies* to a transcendent One, we see more clearly that "social" testimony is one with the spiritual reality to which it testifies. A sustainable life of social witness is built upon that integration.

The prophets of ancient Israel received deep insights into the human condition as they waited upon the Lord in the place where time and eternity meet. They sang, chanted, and wrote poetry of that experience. For example, the prophet Micah lived and prophesied sometime between 750 and 686 BCE. He witnessed a widening gap between rich and poor in the kingdom of Judah, with the variety of social injustices and blights that follow. All this was happening at a time of rising prosperity under a royal-military-priestly establishment. Like the other great prophets, he prophesied that these developments violated God's covenant with Israel. Unless society changed direction, consequences would become only more dire.

Micah reminded rulers and people, "He has told you, O mortal, what is good; and what does the Lord require of you but to do justice, and to love kindness, and to walk humbly with your God?"

(Mic. 6:8). And in one of the most sublime visions of Hebrew scripture, he offered his people a glimpse of their great calling in God's purposes for all humanity:

In the days to come the mountain of the Lord's house shall be established as the highest of the mountains, and shall be raised up above the hills.

Peoples shall stream to it, and many nations shall come and say: "Come, let us go up to the mountain of the Lord, to the house of the God of Jacob; that he may teach us his ways and that we may walk in his paths."

For out of Zion shall go forth instruction, and the word of the Lord from Jerusalem. He shall judge between many peoples, and shall arbitrate between strong nations far away.

They shall beat their swords into plowshares, and their spears into pruning hooks; nation shall not lift up sword against nation, neither shall they learn war any more.

But they shall all sit under their own vines and under their own fig trees, and no one shall make them afraid; for the mouth of the Lord of hosts has spoken.

For all the peoples walk, each in the name of its god, but we will walk in the name of the Lord our God forever and ever.

In that day, says the Lord, I will assemble the lame and gather those who have been driven away, and those whom I have afflicted. The lame I will make the remnant and those who were cast off, a strong nation; and the Lord will reign over them in Mount Zion now and forevermore [Mic. 4:1-7].

Micah's vision deconstructs the royal-military-priestly establishment that had taken control of his people, like all the nations around ancient Judah and Israel. (Indeed, the Israelites had adopted the hierarchical orders of kingship, a military establishment, and a temple-centered worship because of the military threats posed by their neighbors.) If we listen carefully to this prophecy's primary elements, we can hear an integrative vision with timeless, universal power. We can also hear the Quaker vision in an ancient form.

First, we hear of "the mountain of the Lord's house" (Zion, the hill-top site of Jerusalem's temple) thrust above all other mountains (sites where other ancient gods were worshiped). It sounds like a seismic event of outrageous proportions. But such apocalyptic images in Hebrew and Christian Scriptures need decoding. The real "thrust" of this image is a "house" – a "place" of worship that anyone can "see" from anywhere. "Zion" becomes a universal place in *the human heart* where God teaches *all people*. Already this vision subverts Jerusalem's nationalistic temple and its hierocratic priesthood. In his own day, George Fox would draw upon Micah, as well as Daniel and the Gospel of John, when he wrote, "Yea, I say, all the men that come into the world, in Europe, Asia, Africa, and America, Christ enlighteneth every one of them [John 1:9] . . . that with this light they might see him, the great mountain that fills the whole earth [Dan. 2:35], exalted above all the hills and mountains [Mic. 4:1]."[1] As people come to this light within, they come "to know their bodies to be the temples of God and Christ for them to dwell in."[2]

Any real hope for the world depends upon people in all their variety converging at the point of their own direct experience of God, who teaches them in whatever idiom "speaks to their condition." The usual contests of self-interest, power, and religious chauvinism will only perpetuate the cycles of injustice and violence. Micah's prophesy continues with the peoples of the earth converging: "Come, let us go up to the mountain of the Lord . . . that he may teach us his ways and that we may walk in his paths." We find and follow God's teaching *together*. Individual prayer and meditation are important. But we find our way forward together as communities where people of different backgrounds meet on an equal basis.

But Micah's convergence of peoples doesn't simply happen *en masse*. It must begin with a "remnant" (verse 7), often made up of those who are "lame," "cast off," or otherwise "afflicted." For example, in the gospels, those who gathered around Jesus were primarily the dispossessed. Similarly, those who gathered into the early Quaker movement were those most bereft in their hopes to see the kingdom of heaven on earth. The Society of Friends today continues to attract many whose hearts hunger and thirst for peace, justice, and a sustainable world. Liberation theologians today stress God's "preferential option for the poor." That is, God's work in the world begins with and is oriented toward the needs of the poor. Indeed, the poor, and the poor in spirit who align with them, most readily make themselves available to God and to one another. History has shown many times that God is able to do great things through small remnants, minorities consecrated wholeheartedly to divine purposes.

The spiritual convergence of peoples quickly generates *social implications*. Micah envisions a world where God decides and arbitrates conflicts among the peoples. Again, this doesn't require that everyone in the world is already communing with their inward teacher. Small groups and organizations serve as catalytic agents for change as they mediate conflicts, advocate for the poor, and defend the earth. Friends, for example, in tiny numbers — "parts per million," we might say — have been catalysts in this work for 350 years.

This convergence leads on to Micah's sublime vision of *a world without war*. The technologies of war are converted to the technologies of peace and wholesome economic life (in Micah's iron-age poetic imagery, swords and spears are beaten into plowshares and pruning hooks). Moreover, "neither shall they learn war any more": the science and strategies of war are abandoned. This conversion has to begin somewhere. Throughout their history, Friends have been pioneers in mediating international conflict, teaching alternatives to violence, advocating the "peace conversion" of defense-driven economies and technologies, enacting war tax resistance, counterrecruitment, and other initiatives.

Finally, Micah envisions the *economic basis* required to create and sustain a peaceful and just world. When the means of production (vine and fig tree) are in the hands of the people, equity and security build on each other "and none shall make them afraid." In Micah's ancient agrarian imagery, families find security in subsistence farming. He poses this in contrast to the large royal and aristocratic estates farmed by the forced labor of the poor in his day. In effect, Micah affirms, "small is beautiful." That is still a key factor in sustainable economic justice in the twenty-first century.

Cooperatives and collectives, aided by micro-investment and entrepreneurial innovation, build upon that base. Large corporate and financial institutions must be greatly reformed and boundaried. Otherwise, mass exploitation, economic injustice, degradation of the earth, and war will only continue.

Micah's vision is a perennial vision for the destiny of the human race and of all the earth. Prophetic peoples such as the Religious Society of Friends continue to live into that vision, even when they have never read Micah, because it is inscribed in some deep place of the human heart.

Equality and Community among Early Friends

In earliest Quaker faith and practice, equality and community were the warp and weft of a Spirit-led grassroots movement. *Friendship* wove egalitarian relations in a community that struggled against a hostile environment. George Fox's partnership with women such as Elizabeth Hooton, Sarah Blackborow, and Margaret Fell set the general tone for greater equality and creative partnership between women and men in the movement. In 1656 Fox defended the prophetic leadership of Quaker women to Puritan critics:

> *Who is it that dare limit the Holy One of Israel? . . . you are against the scripture, and will not have [Christ] to reign over you; for that male in whom Christ doth reign, rule, and speak, he will own [i.e., recognize] Christ in the female, there to rule, to reign, and speak. . . . Christ is come to reign . . . in the male and in the female.*[3]

Thus, Fox defended women's ministry as divine authority and freedom. But since that authority abides in all persons, the humanistic implications for women's authority and freedom were clear and played out in a variety of more egalitarian social relationships among Friends.

Margaret Fell wrote *Women's Speaking Justified* in 1666, while in prison for hosting Quaker meetings in her home. Her tract is celebrated today as one of the great proto-feminist texts in history. She countered the Puritan misappropriation of Paul's words:

It is said, "I permit not a woman to speak, as saith in the Law"
[1 Cor. 14:34–35]: *but where women are led by the Spirit of
God, they are not under the Law, for Christ in the male and
female is one, and where he is made manifest in male and
female, he may speak. For "he is the end of the Law for righteousness to all them that believe." . . . And so in this true
Church sons and daughters do prophesie* [Joel 2:28; Acts
2:17], *women labour in the Gospel.*[4]

Fell was a central figure in the early movement. Besides being a
prolific writer, she coordinated communications and mentored
traveling Quaker prophets from her home at Swarthmoor Hall in
northwest England. She also administered the Kendal Fund, which
supplied the needs of Friends ministers traveling or suffering in
prison. This kind of mutual aid also enabled poor Friends with prophetic gifts to join the forefront of Quaker expansion. For example,
Mary Fisher, a domestic servant, was among the first to travel to
America and to the Middle East. Early Friends were a strongly
inter-class movement.

In 1658 Fox collaborated with Sarah Blackborow to establish the
Box Meeting, a Quaker women's organization to aid poor and per-
secuted Friends and their families around London. Again, men and
women following the Spirit enacted new patterns that bridged
social class and quickly generalized into a more egalitarian set of
social values and practices.

In 1659 Fox published wide-ranging proposals for reforms in
government. Tithes should be abolished. The legal process should
be reformed to make it more transparent and equitable. Restitution
should replace imprisonment or execution for theft. For the economic empowerment of the poor, Fox advocated that church lands
be parceled out to the poor for farming. Manor houses, church
buildings, and even Whitehall (the government's administrative
headquarters in London) should be converted into almshouses for
the disabled. Fines should go to poor relief, not to the lords of
manors. All forms of patronage should be outlawed.[5]

As the Quaker movement grew and Friends began to prosper,
Fox initiated in 1668 the establishment of schools for boys and for

girls, to educate them "in whatsoever things were civil and useful in the creation."[6] He wrote in 1670 to the newly established quarterly meetings asking that they collect money to aid poor Friends, and to establish poor children in apprenticeships, so they could start a trade. "In all these things the wisdom of God will teach you, by which you may come to help the children of poor Friends, that they may come to rear up their families and preserve them in the fear of God."[7] Clearly, economic empowerment and community interact and promote one another when we let the Spirit lead.

Given this pattern among early Quakers in England, it is astonishing that some Friends adopted slaveholding soon after they emigrated to Barbados in 1656. The practice spread among them as they expanded through the British colonies in America. Like the pacifism of early Friends, equality was the *ethos* of a rapidly expanding, charismatic movement. It had not yet become a thoroughgoing *ethic*. We can only surmise that these early Friends brought an unexamined Eurocentric racism with them to the New World. Fox was deeply disturbed by developments among Friends in Barbados when he visited them in 1671. But they had held slaves for fifteen years already by that time, and manumission was against the laws of the island. For reasons never fully explained, Fox worked to ameliorate slaveholding among Friends, but not to end it. The Barbados case reminds us that the in-group dynamics of *community* can abridge larger questions of *equality*, if the two are not kept in constant conversation.

John Woolman's Vision for Society

As we noted in the preceding chapter, the issue of slavery came to a head among American Friends nearly a century later. John Woolman was a central figure in Philadelphia Yearly Meeting's decision to renounce slaveholding. Sadly, it took another fifty years for American Friends to be clear of slaveholding. But Woolman also wrote more generally on issues of poverty, exploitation, class. and race. *A Plea for the Poor* (1763) is a powerful integration of the issues of economic justice, war, and peace. It places all the issues within the framework of God's creation and sustaining providence:

Our gracious Creator cares and provides for all his creatures. His tender mercies are over all his works; and so far as his love influences our minds, so far we become interested in his workmanship and feel a desire to take hold of every opportunity to lessen the distresses of the afflicted and increase the happiness of the creation. Here we have a prospect of one common interest from which our own is inseparable – that to turn all the treasures we possess into the channel of universal love becomes the business of our lives.

The mind centered in the light sees the wisdom of God in the natural order. The heart turned to the light shares God's compassion for all creatures. We find ourselves in the oneness and common interest of all things and strive to play our part. Woolman continues, showing how this awareness can work among the wealthy:

Men of large estates whose hearts are thus enlarged are like fathers to the poor, and in looking over their brethren in distressed circumstances and considering their own more easy condition, find a field for humble meditation and feel the strength of those obligations they are under to be kind and tender-hearted toward them.

The paternalism implied here is qualified by the humility Woolman enjoins. Meanwhile, generosity spreads among those who benefit from it:

Poor men eased of their burdens and released from too close an application to business are at liberty to hire others to their assistance, to provide well for their animals, and find time to perform those visits amongst their acquaintance which belongs to a well-guided social life.

So the gift of generosity spreads among humans and to the nonhuman creation. In turn, economic sufficiency and empowerment leaven family and social life generally. Thus, *the movement toward greater equity builds community, which in turn strengthens the motives for treating one another more equally.* Woolman concludes, "As the man whose mind is conformed to universal love hath his trust settled in God and finds a firm foundation to stand on in any changes or revolutions that happen amongst men, so also the goodness of his conduct tends to spread a kind, benevolent disposition in the world."[8] Women and men of faith not only *feel* God's universal love; they *trust* God as a present guide and strength to help them act upon that love. That trust is strengthened in community, but extends from there to strangers.

Conversely, Woolman also reflects how inequity and oppression grow gradually over generations, through the accumulation of many small acts of selfishness and thoughtlessness. He concludes:

Thus oppression in the extreme appears terrible, but oppression in more refined appearances remains to be oppression, and where the smallest degree of it is cherished it grows stronger and more extensive: that to labour for a perfect redemption from this spirit of oppression is the great business of the whole family of Christ Jesus in this world.[9]

Note that Woolman focuses on the task of "the whole family of Christ Jesus" as a community of faithful action in the world. He recognized that European Christians had brought the blights of imperial expansion, economic oppression, and careless waste of natural resources to the Americas. These were problems most of all for these communities to solve. But he felt spiritual kinship with non-Christians as well. In 1762 he wrote,

There is a principle which is pure, placed in the human mind, which in different places and ages hath different names; it is, however, pure and proceeds from God ... confined to no forms of religion nor excluded from any where the heart stands in perfect sincerity. In whomsoever this takes root and grows, of what nation soever, they become brethren.[10]

So the work of social redemption bridges differences of religion and culture, forming alliances for peace and justice among those whose hearts are turned toward the pure principle of God.

Finally, Woolman also reflected on the ways oppression and exploitation create the conditions of conflict and war. In his own time and place, he noted how high rents charged by landlords to tenant farmers forced some to leave and press across the frontier, beyond treaty boundaries established with the native tribes. These breaches sparked hostility and war. From such observations, he distilled general principles:

> *Wealth is attended with power, by which bargains and proceedings contrary to universal righteousness are supported; and here oppression, carried on with worldly policy and order, clothes itself with the name of justice and becomes like a seed of discord in the soil; and as this spirit which wanders from the pure habitation prevails, so the seed of war swells and sprouts and grows. . . . Thus comes the harvest spoken of by the prophet [Isa. 17:11], which is "a heap in the day of grief, and of desperate sorrow."*
>
> *Oh, that we who declare against wars and acknowledge our trust to be in God only, may walk in the Light and therein examine our foundation and motives in holding great estates! May we look upon our treasures and the furniture of our houses and the garments in which we array ourselves and try whether the seeds of war have any nourishment in these our possessions or not.*[11]

John Woolman's great ministry was to call Friends and others back to "the pure habitation" of a life grounded in regular communion with God and universal compassion toward all of God's creatures.

The Twentieth Century and Today

There isn't space here for a full history of Quaker insights and action on the issues of equality, economic justice, and peacemaking. (We will return to issues of war and peace in Chapter 7.) But a brief look at one episode from the twentieth century would be useful to place these issues in a more modern framework.

World War I combined capitalist industrial power with new military technologies and nationalist ideologies to wreak death and destruction of an unprecedented scale. Over the nineteenth century, the alienating effects of life in an industrial society had severely degraded the power of communities to nurture spiritual life and foster more equitable social relations. When the crisis came, most churches simply rallied the faithful behind nationalist ideologies and interests. The eighteenth-century insights of John Woolman were still valid at an existential level. But during that war, Friends in Britain realized that Quaker testimony needed to address new macro-economic and military-industrial forces.

After three years of work, London Yearly Meeting approved in 1918 eight "Foundations of a True Social Order." Some features (including sexist language) would be updated by Friends today. But these principles are worth quoting in full, as they set the agenda for Quaker peace and social witness for the rest of the century.

1. The Fatherhood of God, as revealed by Jesus Christ, should lead us toward a brotherhood which knows no restriction of race, sex or social class.

2. This brotherhood should express itself in a social order which is directed, beyond all material ends, to the growth of personality truly related to God and man.

3. The opportunity to full development, physical, moral and spiritual, should be assured to every member of the community, man, woman and child. The development of man's full personality should not be hampered by unjust conditions nor crushed by economic pressure.

4. We should seek for a way of living that will free us from the bondage of material things and mere conventions, that will raise no barrier between man and man, and will put no excessive burden of labour upon any by reason of our superfluous demands.

5. The spiritual force of righteousness, loving-kindness and trust is mighty because of the appeal it makes to the best in every man, and when applied to industrial relations achieves great things.

6. Our rejection of the methods of outward domination, and of the appeal to force, applies not only to international affairs, but to the whole problem of industrial control. Not through

antagonism but through co-operation and goodwill can the best be obtained for each and all.

7. Mutual service should be the principle upon which life is organized. Service, not private gain, should be the motive of all work.

8. The ownership of material things, such as land and capital, should be so regulated as best to minister to the need and development of man.[12]

With these insights, new Quaker organizations were launched in Britain and America to present Quaker social witness to the wider world and to work for social change and peace. Most notably, these included the British Friends Service Council, the American Friends Service Committee, the Friends Committee on National Legislation in Washington, and the Quaker United Nations Offices in Geneva and New York.

The 1950s and 1960s were a high watermark in American Quaker social witness, with many Friends on the vanguard working with the civil rights and antiwar movements, and with others in the beginnings of the women's, gay rights, and environmental movements. Yet by the end of the 1960s, "the revolution came home" (as Quaker activist George Lakey has phrased it). Friends had hitherto focused mainly on social evils "out there." But now they began to ask why, given their advocacy for civil rights and racial integration, were their own meetings not more racially diverse. And in spite of their legacy of early feminism, many Friends struggled with the more radical critiques of patriarchy made by the women's movement. Meanwhile, Friends fumbled at broaching a candid conversation on human sexuality. In the latter twentieth century, Quaker social witness lost some of its outward impetus due to this inward-turning but vital self-examination. That shift is similar to the one John Woolman helped lead among Friends in the latter eighteenth century.

Great progress has been made in the past forty years in updating Quaker feminism and coming to a more open affirmation of homosexual relationships, at least among liberal unprogrammed Friends on both sides of the Atlantic. But race as an internal issue is only beginning to find traction among American Friends. It has not yet been seriously engaged among British Friends. Part of the problem is that race intersects with class, a category still largely submerged in American consciousness, and totemized in British culture. In both cases, unexamined middle-class smugness about education, cultural tastes, and taboos tend to derail sincere white Quaker intentions to reach out to African Americans, Afro-Caribbeans, Latinos, and others who would diversify and enormously enrich the Religious Society of Friends.

In Jesus's day, the Pharisees were more or less a middle-class movement. They were neither the aristocracy that supported the temple priesthood nor "the great unwashed" population of Jewish peasantry. And contact with other races made them ritually unclean. Their elaborate codes of conduct and ritual washings were as much markers of middle-class respectability and racial purity as they were of religious devotion. The teachings of Jesus appealed to many Pharisees. But the way he kept welcoming the poor, the unclean, the social pariahs, and even the occasional Gentile offended Pharisaic class sensibilities perhaps even more than it affronted their religious piety. If we assume the problem for the Pharisees was narrowly a "Jewish" problem, or a "religious" problem, then we have not yet truly heard the gospels. It is partly a class problem, and our problem too.

Equality and Community

Canadian Friend Ursula Franklin reflects,

> *The Light can come from all sides. The joy of experiencing the Light in a completely different way than one has thought it would come is one of the greatest gifts that Friends' meeting for worship has brought me. I believe that meeting for worship has brought the same awareness to all who have seen and understood the message that everyone is equal in the sight of God, that everybody has the capacity to be the vessel of God's word. There is nothing that age, experience and status can do to prejudge where and how the Light will appear.*

This awareness – the religious equality of each and every one – is central to Friends. Early Friends understood this and at the same time they fully accepted the inseparable unity of life, and spoke against the setting apart of the secular and the sacred. It was thus inevitable that religious equality would be translated into the equality of everyday social behaviour. Friends' testimony to plain speech and plain dress was both a testimony of religious equality and a testimony of the unacceptability of all other forms of inequality.[13]

Again, deep insight into our true *equality* is born of worship and life in *community*. Communities of sustained commitment to one another and to purposes that transcend themselves not only experience equality among themselves. They also work to establish equality more widely in society. This typically takes the form of aid to those in need, work for economic empowerment, and advocacy for the equal rights and opportunities of all.

Laws ensuring equal rights and opportunities are vital to a just society. But equality as such is an empty, formal concept. Without a shared life within a horizon of meaning that transcends us all, questions of equality quickly become matters of contention, rivalry, resentment, and strife. A shared religious language and a consecration to divine purposes in the world are crucial to maintaining community. Otherwise, rivalry and contention – identity politics – rend the fabric of fellowship. When the apostle Paul saw early Christians divided by identity politics he reminded them, "there is no longer Jew or Greek, there is no longer slave or free, there is no longer male and female; for all of you are one in Christ Jesus.... For freedom Christ has set us free. Stand firm, therefore, and do not submit again to a yoke of slavery" (Gal. 3:27-28; 5:1). Affirmation of our different identities and equal rights is important and empowering to a degree. But without a countervailing conviction of our common humanity and divine calling, it divides and enslaves us.

Yes, we retain our natural and cultural inheritances. We are *both* this *and* that. But as noted in Chapter 2, we also grow in the light to become a new creation that is *neither* this *nor* that. Liberated from pride and resentment, from justifying ourselves and judging others, we are freed to serve God by serving others. Paul, who had once proudly counted himself "a Hebrew of the Hebrews" (Phil. 3:5), found this radical freedom modeled in the life of Jesus, "who, though he was in the form of God, did not regard equality with God as something to be grasped, but emptied himself, taking the form of a servant, being born in human likeness" (Phil. 2:6-7, RSV). That same divine wisdom animated the early and traditional Quaker testimony of equality and community.

African American Quaker historian Emma Lapsansky captures this sense of joyful liberation when she suggests,

> *If we can stay focused on social justice as something that will bring us pleasure, not just a sense of righteousness, and if we can remember that social justice is a bit like housework – no matter how well you do it, it just has to be done again; and perhaps most important, if we can keep our sense of humor, then we have a good chance to be carried over those places where it seems God has abandoned us.*[14]

We are carried over those places most often through our fellowship with others in the faithful struggle.

Equality and community are two threads in the seamless garment of Quaker testimony. They continually cross in the warp and weft of faithful lives. Their relationship is dialogical, not in the sense of being opposites, but in the way they continue to qualify one another. If an emphasis on equality by itself is prone to resentment and contention, an emphasis on community without equality easily lapses into sentimentality. By itself, pursued for its own sake, community becomes merely affective and loses accountability. Emotional appeals to community may even gloss over hidden agendas and perpetuate inequality or exclusion.

The dynamic unity of equality and community breaks down when the community loses focus on its commitment to be a servant to divine purposes. That is, it loses its social and spiritual transcendence. The community turns in on itself, and ideological dualisms dominate the conversation. In some Quaker meetings and institutions, the dualism is cast between "hierarchy" and an undifferentiated unity. Individuals and groups taking initiative and leading in some direction are accused of seeking power and hierarchical authority. It is argued that everyone should weigh in on every decision. Important new initiatives may be neutralized and gifted leaders drift away. Middle-class groups are particularly prone to these free-floating moods of suspicion and resentment.

What is usually missing in these stalemated conversations is the concept of *heterarchy*, in which people with different gifts, abilities, and concerns are empowered by the whole group to carry out certain tasks. These individuals and groups remain accountable to the group as a whole, which retains oversight over all activities undertaken in its name. But in general, the meeting lets them get on with their work, their service to the meeting and beyond. Paul's image (in 1 Cor. 12) of the Church as the spiritual body of Christ, with various members endowed with various functions, describes well the heterarchical dynamics of a Spirit-led group that differentiates organically into its different tasks. Again, equality and community are not static states of being. They are processes that interact and participate in the larger mystery of the kingdom (realm, or "kindom") of heaven on earth.

In the following chapter we will see how both equality and community are foundational to the processes of group spiritual discernment. We will also examine how various forms of leadership in the meeting can nurture Spirit-led decision making in the whole group.

Advices and Queries from Britain Yearly Meeting's *Quaker Faith & Practice*

#33: Are you alert to practices here and throughout the world which discriminate against people on the basis of who or what they are or because of their beliefs? Bear witness to the humanity of all people, including those who break society's conventions or its laws. Try to discern new growing points in social and economic life. Seek to understand the causes of injustice, social unrest and fear. Are you working to bring about a just and compassionate society which allows everyone to develop their capacities and fosters the desire to serve?

#17: Do you respect that of God in everyone though it may be expressed in unfamiliar ways or be difficult to discern? Each of us has a particular experience of God and each must find the way to be true to it. When words are strange or disturbing to you, try to sense where they come from and what has nourished the lives of others. Listen patiently and seek the truth which other people's opinions may contain for you. Avoid hurtful criticism and provocative language. Do not allow the strength of your convictions to betray you into making statements or allegations that are unfair or untrue. Think it possible that you may be mistaken.

#18: How can we make the meeting a community in which each person is accepted and nurtured, and strangers are welcome? Seek to know one another in the things which are eternal; bear the burden of each other's failings and pray for one another. As we enter with tender sympathy into the joys and sorrows of each other's lives, ready to give help and to receive it, our meeting can be a channel for God's love and forgiveness.

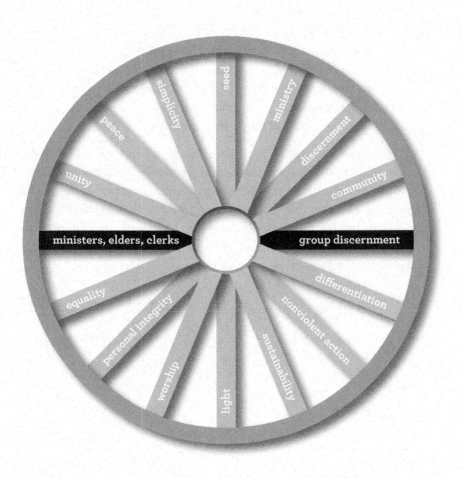

CHAPTER 5

The Peaceable Kingdom

We continue to discover the organic, interlocking whole of Quaker faith and practice. More than "this, that and the other thing," Quaker testimony and spiritual discipline integrate a person into an "I" that beholds and addresses other human and nonhuman creatures as "thou." We come to "know one another in that which is eternal," in the One, the "Thou" who addresses us and heals us at the deepest places of our being. Thus, we shall see in this chapter how equality and community interact to form the foundation for one of the most celebrated aspects of Quaker faith and practice: "decisions made in unity," Friends searching for God's will in the matters of their life together, rather than resorting to votes.

But here we will discover yet another paradox: this most egalitarian and inclusive form of decision making requires a sensitivity and mutual rapport that must be *nurtured* by gifted, experienced *leaders*. The recognition and encouragement of leadership in the meeting exists in creative tension with our more spontaneous, improvised mode of seeking unity in the light. In other words, in any given process of decision making, we are all beginners, starting afresh. But some have begun afresh more times, have learned from those experiences, have steeped themselves in the Quaker traditions, and can help the group avoid the pitfalls of self-interest, short-sightedness, and impetuosity. At the same time, however, these leaders are answerable to the group. The group helps leaders avoid the pitfalls of, well, leadership. This is a complex process of life together, but it is the only path to a sustainable life — a life that sustains the Friends meeting, as the Friends meeting helps build a sustainable world.

Friends today place an enormous weight of expectation on our "Quaker process" of decision making. But many will acknowledge that the process is deteriorating from lack of shared understanding of what the process is and how to participate faithfully in it. Under these circumstances, meetings easily resort to "the art of the possible," an agreement to disagree and a search for convenient options everyone can live with. This deterioration is directly linked to the attenuation of leadership among Friends. This situation is *unsustainable*. It produces a comfortable but unchallenging atmosphere that will not rise to the prophetic task of our time.

An amoeba is a formless one-celled creature that functions well enough in its own simple way. But with greater size and complexity, plants and animals had to evolve a variety of internal forms and functions: tissues, organs, members, and so on. Near the end of the preceding chapter, we noted the organic image of the body that Paul utilized in describing different forms and functions within the body of Christ, based on the variety of spiritual gifts in the group. In the individualistic culture of our times, we may try to function as amoebas without any particular form or function other than our own personal purposes. But as a religious body, the Friends meeting and the larger Friends bodies within which it functions must differentiate internally into some basic forms of leadership with particular functions in service to the whole, according to the spiritual gifts that manifest themselves among its members.

Edward Hicks and *The Peaceable Kingdom*

Edward Hicks was a recorded minister among Friends in Bucks County, Pennsylvania, during the early nineteenth century. As a boy, he was apprenticed to a sign painter and developed some basic skills in pictorial painting. Hicks was highly esteemed as a Friends minister, but also carried on a sideline of painting. Early and traditional Friends rejected music and the arts as vain pastimes affordable mainly among the wealthy. Nevertheless, Hicks painted all his life. His grand theme was the prophecy of Isaiah 11:

The wolf shall live with the lamb, the leopard shall lie down with the kid, the calf and the lion and the fatling together, and

a little child shall lead them. The cow and the bear shall graze, their young shall lie down together, and the lion shall eat straw like the ox. The nursing child shall play over the hole of the asp, and the weaned child shall put his hand on the adder's den. They will not hurt or destroy on all my holy mountain; for the earth will be full of the knowledge of the Lord as the waters cover the sea [11:6–9].

Hicks painted as many as one hundred versions of Isaiah's vision. He called them "The Peaceable Kingdom."

We know how Edward Hicks understood Isaiah's prophecy, from a listener's shorthand record of a sermon he preached in 1837 at the Goose Creek Friends Meeting in Virginia. There he presents the different animals as different human personality types, reconciled in the love that comes from direct knowledge of God. He interprets the four predators as representing imbalances in the four bodily humors, as described in medieval medicine. The bear represents the phlegmatic, or stubborn, personality. The wolf represents the melancholy personality. The leopard represents the sanguine personality, which Hicks associates with sensuality, luxury, and cruelty. Finally, the lion is choleric, given to anger. In a similar way, George Fox had associated imbalances in human behavior with various animals.[1] These "natures" are appropriate to those particular animals, but inappropriate for us. In humans they "put nature out of its course." Today we do not subscribe to medieval and folk ideas about bodily humors as the source of personality. But we do well to remember that we are embodied souls. There are physical dimensions to our psychological temperaments and spiritual struggles.

Hicks viewed himself as a lion, for he struggled with anger. This was a problem particularly during the 1820s when his cousin, Elias Hicks, was the center of controversy among American Friends, leading to the first major schism in Quaker history. Edward had strong feelings on behalf of his embattled cousin. These emotions sometimes interfered with the exercise of his gift in vocal ministry, which must proceed from the Spirit of peace and compassion. Hicks recognized that he needed more patience, a trait he associated with the ox in Isaiah's vision. He had been comforted and mentored by an elder in his meeting who embodied that temperament. He mentions this man in the sermon:

> The most valuable father in the church of Christ I ever knew was a man of choleric complexion, and in his first nature like a lion; but when I knew him he was patient, submissive, and powerful as an ox. He was truly a precious father, taking me by the hand in my youth, and leading by precept and example.[2]

So for Hicks, Isaiah's exotic prophecy was not otherworldly. It was fulfilled in his own Quaker community. He kept painting his Peaceable Kingdoms as a method of meditation on his own experience and as a sign of hope to others.

Edward Hicks's vision of the Peaceable Kingdom sets out the dynamic elements to be considered in this chapter. Quaker group discernment and decision making rely upon the faith that our different personalities can be reconciled and brought into peaceful unity in the light of God's love. This chapter explores the Quaker tradition of group spiritual discernment: seeking God's will together — making decisions in unity, without voting. But that unity does not just happen. To become adept at finding unity together, four key elements are necessary.

First, all channels must be open for the Spirit's leading of the group. That is, all must share *equally* in the right and responsibility to speak the truth as the Spirit may lead them in the moment. Second, all must share equally the right and responsibility to remain silent unless they feel led to contribute something helpful to the group's discernment. The Spirit needs space to work in the group. Third, the group must function as a community, ready to be reconciled into one body, to overcome differences and hurts. Finally, if it is to develop these first three capacities, the meeting needs leadership — the shepherding, encouraging and nurturing efforts of gifted clerks, elders, and ministers. As noted in the preceding chapter, the Spirit-led body is heterarchical. It requires the diligent work of variously gifted individuals and committees. When all these elements come together, we find our individual insights and contributions raised to another level, often beyond what any of us could have imagined or achieved. As in Isaiah's timeless vision, we find ourselves together at peace on God's "holy mountain."

The Meeting for Business

As noted in Chapter 2, early Friends believed they were moved by "the same Spirit the prophets and apostles were in." Accordingly, they patterned their decision making after the example they found in the New Testament church. For example, at a key meeting in Jerusalem, "the apostles and the elders, with the consent of the whole church" discerned that it "seemed good to the Holy Spirit and to us" to approve Paul's work in spreading the gospel to the gentile world (Acts 15:22, 28). Later in that first century, the apostle John warned his congregations, "Beloved, do not believe every spirit, but test the spirits to see whether they are from God" (1 John 4:1). Similarly, Paul encouraged early Christians to speak as the Spirit led, but urged congregations to listen with discernment: "Do not quench the Spirit. Do not despise prophecies, but test everything; hold fast to what is good; abstain from every form of evil" (1 Thess. 5:19-22). Jesus instructed his followers to work out conflicts between themselves: "For where two or three are gathered in my name, I am there among them" (Matt. 18:20).

Edward Burrough gives us the clearest description of early Quaker decision making. His 1662 advice to Friends in London contains many elements still important to Quaker process today:

> *Being orderly come together [you are] not to spend time with needless, unnecessary and fruitless discourses; but to proceed in the wisdom of God, not in the way of the world, as a worldly assembly of men, by hot contests, by seeking to outspeak and over-reach one another in discourse as if it were controversy between party and party of men, or two sides violently striving for dominion, not deciding affairs by the greater vote. But in the wisdom, love and fellowship of God, in gravity, patience, meekness, and unity and concord, submitting one to another in lowliness of heart, and in the holy Spirit of truth and righteousness all things to be carried on; by hearing, and determining every matter coming before you, in love, coolness, gentleness and dear unity; I say as one only party, all for the truth of Christ, and for the carrying on of the work of the Lord, and assisting one another in whatsoever ability God hath given.*[3]

Notice all the qualitative words used to describe the state in which Spirit-led decisions are made: love, lowliness of heart, humility, gentleness, coolness, patience, gravity. In contrast to the *quantitative* measurement of agreement utilized in voting, Quaker decision making takes place through the *shared discernment* of a *qualitative* state of being in the group. Where "dear unity" is sensed on a given matter, the meeting feels clear to move ahead with a course of action. (It is revealing that in traditional parliamentary usage, a vote is called a "division.")

That spiritual sense of unity is grounded first of all in the group's ongoing experience of worship. The meeting for business is an extension of the meeting for worship. Experience in offering vocal ministry in the meeting for worship trains us in knowing when and how to contribute to an item for consideration in the meeting for business, even if the manner of speaking may be different.

Thus, Quaker decision-making is profoundly different, not only from voting but also from a mere compromise or consensus among human viewpoints:

> *In our meetings for worship we seek through the stillness to know God's will for ourselves and for the gathered group. Our meetings for church affairs, in which we conduct our business, are also meetings for worship based on silence, and they carry the same expectation that God's guidance can be discerned if we are truly listening together and to each other, and are not blinkered by preconceived opinions. It is this belief that God's will can be recognized through the discipline of silent waiting which distinguishes our decision-making process from the secular idea of consensus. We have a common purpose in seeking God's will through waiting and listening, believing that every activity of life should be subject to divine guidance.*[4]

Participants in such a business process must be constantly mindful of their motivations. Through "inward recollection" participants avoid trying to have their way, but seek a higher synthesis of individual insights. Howard Brinton observes:

> *Eloquence which appeals to emotion is out of place. Those who come to the meeting not so much to discover Truth as to win acceptance of their opinions may find that their views carry little weight. Opinions should always be expressed humbly and tentatively in the realization that no one person sees the whole Truth and that the whole meeting can see more of Truth than can any part of it.*[5]

While there are some inevitable "dos and don'ts," like those mentioned in the last two quotations, the Quaker meeting for business cannot be reduced to a matter of etiquette or technique. Again, the inward quality of being is most crucial to discern. Particular questions to be resolved by the group are discerned from that place.

William Taber calls that collective place "the Mind of Christ." His qualitative description is worth quoting at length here:

> *A business meeting in touch with the Mind of Christ may seem to go more slowly, but may actually get more done in the end. In this state of consciousness, an individual or meeting tends first of all to contemplate or to "absorb" a new idea or concern for a period of time without judging it or reacting to it, until someone feels a clear inward motion about it. Spiritual discernment seems to flourish best from this contemplative, reflective, nonlinear state of mind, which is a wide, non-judgmental, almost non-attached, but very alert attentiveness.*
>
> *However, being in the Mind of Christ does not mean being "spaced out," for the analytical faculties are not suppressed; they are merely put into their rightful harmony by being surrounded and cushioned by a much vaster mind, which takes all things into account. Indeed, our analytical faculties are at least as sharp, if not sharper, in the Mind of Christ than they are at other times; the difference is that here we know that we are not just our surface mind, as we Westerners tend to assume, and the difference is that this surface mind is no longer the master, but the tool, of the more integrated person we become in the Mind of Christ.*[6]

Some of Taber's language here is very similar to his description of the meeting for worship (see Chapter 2). For example, just as he writes of entering the "stream" of Quaker worship, he also describes the "stream of Quaker process." It is "always moving, always changing, yet it is the same stream. We step into the same stream that George Fox entered."[7] Ultimately, Quaker process is not a set of procedures to enact, but a larger reality in which we participate together. Some Friends use the term "gathered" to describe either the meeting for worship or the meeting for business when it reaches that transcendent state.

In both worship and business, Taber suggests that the meeting benefits from a significant core of Friends who practice daily devotion to prayer and meditation in the Spirit.[8] Without that anchoring, the meeting can easily fall into merely analytical and pragmatic thinking at best, factions, power struggles, and resentments at worst. Michael Sheeran suggests that this worshipful state makes the difference between decisions that reach a higher synthesis and those that simply find the lowest common denominator of workable agreement.[9] He suggests that Quaker faith and practice centers in the "primacy of the event," those found moments of deeper unity. His research in Philadelphia Yearly Meeting found that "Christocentrics and certain universalists" most commonly know to look for and discern the gathered moment. These Friends appear to be more motivated to reconsider their own preferences, more likely to feel obligated to unite with decisions reached in that atmosphere. Those who do not understand or perceive the gathered moment are more prone to speak in terms of "good process," democratic values, or social action.[10]

Taber identifies five "gut-feelings" that attend the meeting for business. More than one may be felt simultaneously. First, there is the *joy of being together* as a community generally liberated from prejudice, fear, and loneliness. Second, there is the *joy of being with God*, our Great Friend, who feels like a place of cool and quiet. Third, there is *assurance*, the sense of being upheld by the divine: being tendered and gentled, as the boundaries of the self are blurred. Fourth, there is *trust* — both in God and in the process — that grows with practice. Finally, there is *excitement* "as we come face to face with the utter unpredictability of God at work through our lives. As we enter, we never know what will happen!"[11]

Through and beyond these gut feelings, real business, real decision making takes place. Business meeting in the manner of Friends could be compared to a card game, where no one tries to win, but a larger success is sought together by the group. Moreover, what constitutes "success" with a given item of business may not be fully known at the outset by any of the participants. Each participant has been dealt certain "cards," particular insights and experiences that may bear on the matter at hand. An item of business often comes to the meeting for business from a committee, whose members have already given this matter considerable time and attention. Their cards are mostly played as the item for decision is first introduced. But details or insights that did not seem important to share at the outset may prove crucial as the discussion develops. Other participants in the process may add useful questions or comments along the way, perhaps altering the entire frame of consideration. But each person must prayerfully consider *whether* and *when* it is appropriate to play a card. The aim of speaking is usefulness, generosity of spirit, and efficient brevity – not self-expression. Hence, seasoned Friends often participate with a certain poker-faced demeanor to aid in the shared search for truth.

Burrough's "dear unity" is not always easy to find. Sometimes a matter must be "laid over" to the next meeting, to season it further in the hearts of participants. Further reflection and perhaps more committee work may bring the question to a more satisfactory answer. But the group may find unity in a decision that some cannot unite with. Here the difference between Spirit-led decisions and voting becomes still more apparent. Those who find themselves out of unity with the decision do not quantify their number and become a bloc of opposition. Rather, they express their qualitative sense that the group has found unity by ignoring something vital. In that case, they may speak up to "stand aside" from that unity. By so doing, they allow the meeting to move ahead with that decision.

But if they feel the proposed action could be harmful, they may "stand in the way" of the decision. The group must take seriously their discomfort with the decision. Often it is good to lay the matter over to the next meeting and see if time and further conversation helps. The meeting may move ahead with a decision, even if individuals refuse to stand aside, if members feel the individuals are not acting in good faith. But that step is taken with trepidation. Moreover, if a meeting makes many decisions with Friends standing aside, trust will begin to erode. Older, unresolved issues or deeper divisions may be festering below the surface and require careful work by seasoned Friends.[12]

"Dear unity" does not just happen spontaneously, unerringly, and always. It must be nurtured by three key forms of leadership, three kinds of catalytic agents at work in the life of the meeting: clerks, elders, and ministers.

Clerks

The role of the clerk is to help the body move, to shepherd the group through the decisions it faces. The clerk of the meeting is not a facilitator, who guides a group through a premeditated set of exercises toward a chosen goal. The clerk does not know where the body should go, but coordinates the process of the body learning where God wants it to go, and how. As Sheeran describes it, the role of the clerk is "a combination of the ability to read the community's attitudes and to lead the community to new unity."[13] But that is also the role of *any participant* who speaks in the meeting for business. As implied by the metaphor of the card game, one speaks according to one's reading of the group's need and the right time to supply that need. So the clerk simply has a particularly strong and developed gift in doing what everyone else in the meeting needs to do in the meeting's process. The clerk's gift — or rather, God's gift to the meeting through that person — comes to its highest moment in discerning the gathering unity of the group and giving it clear expression by proposing a written minute. Then it is the shared discernment of the group to recognize the rightness of that minute, modify it, or reject it. Throughout the process, each participant is both a reader and a leader in the meeting. The process is most successful when we share a sense of being led by a divine guide whose wisdom is beyond all of us.

Douglas Steere describes the role of the clerk thus:

He or she is a good listener, has a clear mind that can handle issues, has the gift of preparing a written minute that can succinctly sum up the sense of the meeting, and is one who has faith in the presuppositions that were mentioned earlier: faith in the presence of a Guide; faith in the deep revelatory genius of such a meeting to arrive at a decision that may break new ground and yet may in fresh ways be in keeping with the Society of Friends' deepest testimonies; and faith in each of those present being potentially the vehicle of the fresh resolving insight. With all of this, a good clerk is a person who refuses to be hurried and can weary out dissension with a patience borne of the confidence that there is a way through, although the group may have to return again and again to the issue before clearness comes and a proper decision is reached.[14]

These traits of a clerk are most visible during the meeting for business. But equally important is the work she or he performs between meetings. There is much consultation and patient listening to be done in preparation for and in following up each meeting. The clerk must understand the intentions of committees bringing business to the meeting. The clerk must design the meeting agenda appropriately to the business at hand. The clerk must follow up after meeting with individuals or groups at odds with each other or with the emerging unity. These are just some of the activities of a good clerk.

But perhaps most importantly, the clerk must be vigilant in maintaining a worshipful, reverent sense in the meeting for business. If the meeting grows divisive or simply loses focus, a few moments spent in quiet reflection and prayer may save the group from much longer tangents or even mutual alienation. The flock knows the voice of its true shepherd (John 10:11–18), who alone can lead in unity and divine wisdom. But the clerk can be a helpful catalyst through the process. As Friends have traditionally understood it, Quaker business method is not itself the leading of the Spirit, any more than silence is the aim of Quaker worship. It is a way of conducting ourselves that creates the space among us for the Spirit to lead.

Elders

The clerk alone cannot see or respond to all the confusions, misunderstandings, and divergences within the meeting. Unity must be nurtured more broadly by elders. The role of eldership among Friends is generally to nurture the "right ordering" of meeting life. It is thus primarily a concern for the body of the meeting. But that naturally entails the nurture of individuals and their part in the body. In a religious society radically committed to following the

Spirit, the potential is great for delusion and wishful thinking to throw matters into confusion. Those with more experience in discerning the Spirit's leading (whether older in years or not) are crucial as mentors to individuals and as anchors to the life of the meeting.

This form of leadership has appeared among Friends from the beginning. In 1653 William Dewsbury wrote to the first meetings established in the North of England, suggesting that they choose one or two "most grown in the Power and Life, in pure discerning in the Truth, to take the care and charge over the Flock of God in that place." This was informal eldership, leadership mainly through personal guidance and lived example. They were to see that meetings were held regularly and in good order. When individuals were not living up to the standards of Friends, Dewsbury recommended plain speaking. Early Friends could be sternly confrontational with individuals they felt were dishonest or hypocritical. But where a person was truly open, Dewsbury advised tenderness and patience: "Wash the Disciples Feet in bowing to the pure in the least appearance, and ministering to it . . . then you will have union together."[15]

As the movement developed, eldership became more formally established. Some had misgivings about this development. In the 1660s George Bishop warned that official eldership could "place the Thing to the Person, and not the Person to the Thing." That is, true eldership is exercised wherever that gift is found in the meeting. Official roles may encourage those who are ungifted and discourage those who are truly gifted but not recognized.[16] Bishop's warning is worth remembering. Formal eldership can cause us to ignore the variety of ways in which a variety of individuals nurture the meeting. Like clerkship, eldership names a gift that stands out in some, but is always more widely exercised in the meeting.

On the other hand, individuals are often challenged to develop their gifts more intentionally when the responsibility of a formal role is placed upon them. Beatrice Saxon Snell, an esteemed Friend in Britain Yearly Meeting (d. 1982) tells a useful story:

> I had a salutary lesson in sober thinking when I was first asked
> to become an elder. The invitation appalled me . . . I read up

the appropriate passages in [Faith & Practice] and felt still more appalled. Nevertheless I had been in the Society just long enough to know that the group often has a wisdom which can seldom be justified on logical grounds but which is, nevertheless, superior to the wisdom of the individual. I therefore went to consult a much respected elder of my acquaintance. She . . . let me talk myself out. When I had quite finished she inclined herself slightly towards me and said: "My dear, we have to take what we can get." I have since been convinced that this is a text which ought to be framed and hung up over the bed of every elder in the Society: it ought to be hung over the bed of every Friend who is tempted to refer to the elders as "they."[17]

Ministers

The Quaker movement was founded by a band of approximately sixty or seventy itinerant prophets. These women and men converged with George Fox's message and spiritual counsel. Quaker faith and practice began to take shape through their leadership. Part of that leadership was to identify useful experiments they found among meetings they visited, and to spread their usage among Friends. Like eldership, ministry was a gift that meetings came to recognize ("record") formally in some men and women. These persons were unpaid and had no formal training, but took ministry seriously as a calling, a vocation. That is, they organized their lives around service to Friends through the exercise of that gift.

Until the twentieth century, meetings depended primarily upon the vocal ministry, teaching, and spiritual guidance of these recorded ministers in their midst. As we have already observed with clerks and elders, the gift of prophetic vocal ministry was by no means limited to these individuals. But the gift was discerned more clearly, and was developed with greater personal devotion, in some. Ministers were recognized in part for their insight into spiritual "conditions" of Friends in the meeting, and for their ability to speak prophetically to the times. But they were also bearers of the

Quaker tradition. They studied the Bible and the literature of past generations of Friends, along with other useful literature. Besides leadership in their own meeting, ministers also traveled in ministry, visiting other meetings. This arduous work cross-fertilized the Religious Society of Friends and kept spiritual renewal moving through the body.[18]

Over time, the traditional practice of ministry shifted in diverging directions among Friends (see the next chapter for more historical overview). In the latter nineteenth century, evangelical renewal led some American Friends to replace traditional Quaker ministers with "released" (paid) pastors. Meanwhile, more liberal Friends dropped the formal recognition of ministers in the early twentieth century. The smaller stream of Conservative Friends held to traditional practices. But on the whole, as Friends were increasingly influenced by other churches and by various cultural currents, traditional understandings of Quaker faith and practice began to disperse. The meeting's sense of who was particularly gifted in ministry consequently became debatable. A few outstanding leaders, such as Rufus Jones, were able to shape a degree of consensus among many Friends. But that was primarily through publication and public speaking, not the more personal forms of encounter exercised by traditional ministers. The absence of a vocational sense of ministry among Friends has placed greater stress upon elders and clerks to nurture unity in group discernment. As a result, the resort to lowest denominator decisions becomes harder to resist. Edward Hicks's Peaceable Kingdom easily becomes a community of porcupines, giving one another plenty of leeway.

Still, on the local meeting level, to this day, some individuals are always recognized as particularly gifted in vocal ministry, in spiritual counsel, and in the ability to interpret the times. And in some yearly meetings formal recording of ministers has been revived, in recognition of those whose gifts and dedication are too clear to be ignored.

For many Friends today, living in our highly individualistic culture, it has become difficult to trust that these roles of leadership are in service to the body, and not an opportunity to repress individuality or to dominate the meeting. Certainly, individual clerks, elders, and ministers may at times need to be reminded of that true meaning of their gift. But without these three forms of catalytic leadership, the meeting for business will increasingly fail.[19]

Coherence of identity and purpose require a *shared language within the community*. The prophetic Christian roots of Quaker faith and practice provide that shared language. That is not to say that *individuals* should not learn a second, third, or fourth spiritual language that helps them grow spiritually. In a multicultural society we are enriched by these interfaith and cross-cultural conversations and borrowings. Even George Fox had personal interest in some ideas associated with Rosicrucian and Hermetic philosophy. He studied the Koran at one point in his life. While he apparently spoke of these things in conversation with some individuals, his ministry in spoken and written word among meetings was consistently in the widely shared biblical code he knew could forge and sustain unity. Friends today urgently need to recognize this differentiation of levels between personal and community life. We can bring other traditions into the meeting conversation, often with real benefit. But we need to regain fluency the prophetic Christian "first language" of Quaker faith and practice if we are to sustain productive conversation together.

Reflections: The Body and Its Antibodies

The "body-life" of Friends is something we hold together in trust. As we have noted a few times in these chapters, we are children both of a transcendent God and of the whole universe. Consequently, our meetings for worship and our meetings for business take place at that juncture between our lives as natural creatures and our emerging new creation in the Spirit. The "body" or "mind" of Christ is held in that conjoint reality. That body therefore manifests traits in common with our physical bodies. For example, our physical bodies are held in a sustainable integrity by the work of multiple immune systems that constantly identify and counter alien bodies that would otherwise sicken and even kill the body. Various antibodies thus preserve the health of the body. Clerks, elders, and ministers function something like these multiple immune systems of the body, identifying and countering spiritual forces that can sicken and even kill the body. That is, they help members see where their thinking is confused, their motives are mixed, their emotions "hooked," or their personal interests unexamined.

The Movement for a New Society, founded in the early 1970s, was one of the most prophetic off-shoots from American Friends in the past half-century. Yet it began to stagnate in the 1980s. Many living in its shared-living houses in Philadelphia felt that community life was more important than prophetic witness to the wider society. In addition, efforts by MNS leaders to develop new analyses and strategies to challenge the neo-conservative politics of that decade were discounted by many in MNS as middle-class intellectualizing and patriarchal self-importance. Looking back, Quaker activist and MNS co-founder George Lakey reflects, "I think one of the reasons that MNS isn't still around is the downside of consensus. . . . Consensus can be valuable for encouraging unity. In the longer-run, however, consensus can be a conservative influence, stifling prospects of organizational change."[20] Again, we confront the question of sustainability. Can Friends today claim to be free of this problem?

———————————●———————————

This chapter has lifted up the role of leadership, both recognized and informal, in helping meetings to find dynamic, productive unity together. Leadership must always maintain as its purpose the unity, coherence, and sustainability of the body, the community. When that happens, leadership will perform a servant role and not compromise the equality of dignity and voice among Friends. Hence, group spiritual discernment among Friends is the pre-eminent practice through which the testimonies of equality and community maintain their dynamic balance.

The formal name "Religious Society of Friends" did not arise until the 1790s. But the term "society" applies most properly to a people grounded in a particular set of practices and ways of knowing. The sociologist Max Weber defines "society" as a set of interactions based upon intentions that are in turn founded upon a common body of knowledge, norms, customs, and expectations. All these are highly developed in Quaker faith and practice, creating a religious society at some distance from the social norms around it. The development of Quaker organization beginning in the 1660s parallels the founding of the Royal Society among early modern scientists at the same time. In their different ways, both societies worked to define radically new processes and systems of accountability for the investigation of truth. These parallels testify not only to the powerful syntheses that occurred in the seventeenth century, but also to the intimate affinities between spiritual and material reality, which this book continues to explore under a concern for a sustainable life on the earth.

The Welsh Seeker William Erbury presciently defined the Quaker religious sensibility in 1652 (though he died before encountering Friends): "Admission [in the formal churches] intimates the Church of Christ to be a corporation, as if there were a common council among them, whereas the [true] Church is a free company or society of friends, who come together, not as called by an outward [authority] but freely choosing by the inward spirit."[21]

Advices and Queries from Britain Yearly Meeting's *Quaker Faith & Practice*

#14: Are your meetings for church affairs held in a spirit of worship and in dependence on the guidance of God? Remember that we do not seek a majority decision nor even consensus. As we wait patiently for divine guidance our experience is that the right way will open and we shall be led into unity.

#15: Do you take part as often as you can in meetings for church affairs? Are you familiar enough with our church government to contribute to its disciplined processes? Do you consider the difficult questions with an informed mind as well as a generous and loving spirit? Are you prepared to let your insights and personal wishes take their place alongside those of others or be set aside as the meeting seeks the right way forward? If you cannot attend, uphold the meeting prayerfully.

#18: How can we make the meeting a community in which each person is accepted and nurtured, and strangers are welcome? Seek to know one another in the things which are eternal, bear the burden of each other's failings and pray for one another. As we enter with tender sympathy into the joys and sorrows of each other's lives, ready to give help and to receive it, our meeting can be a channel for God's love and forgiveness.

#20: Do you give sufficient time to sharing with others in the meeting, both newcomers and long-time members, your understanding of worship, of service, and of commitment to the Society's witness? Do you give a right proportion of your money to support Quaker work?

CHAPTER 6

Tragedy and Renewal in Quaker History

It has proved impossible for Friends to hold together the powerful synthesis of Quaker faith and practice we have followed thus far. Various forces have pulled Friends apart over 350 years. Separations have been acrimonious, especially for a Religious Society of *Friends* so strongly grounded in an ethic of peace and unity. There is no denying the tragic losses to all "Children of the Light" as they have fought over the legacy of their spiritual fathers and mothers. Dividing from one another, they also divided the inheritance and lost the rich integrity of Quaker faith and practice. Opting for one side or another of our perplexing but energizing paradoxes, Friends have reframed their faith and practice by combining it with the beliefs and practices of other traditions. As they made "Quakerism" (a coinage that became popular by the early twentieth century) more accessible to seekers and newcomers, the deeper registers of traditional faith and practice became opaque and uninteresting to Friends. In other words, the unique "Society" of Quaker ways of knowing truth and being in the world have blended with the ways of the wider society.

Nevertheless, it is also true that these diverging streams of Friends have produced recombinant forms, hybrids with new vigor and outreach to the wider society. These Quaker renewals have been engendered by Friends "marrying out" from the Quaker fold, both literally and theologically. New Quaker varieties have moved into new niches in the social ecology, pioneering new fields of service and witness, sometimes with impressive growth as well. The genetic principles implied here are not purely metaphorical. As we have observed repeatedly in these chapters, we are both natural creatures and part an emerging new creation. Our Quaker odyssey participates not only in the Spirit's movements, but in the natural processes of organic evolution as well.

Consider the story of the Fall. Genesis 3 narrates in mythic terms a tragic loss of primal unity between man, woman, creation, and God. But in that story we can also recognize the *felix culpa* ("happy sin") of human development toward a higher consciousness. Tragedy, in the ancient Greek sense, is an event that both wounds and ennobles us. As in the cross of Jesus, tragedy devastates but also raises us — if we have the eyes to see and the arms to stretch to its painful paradoxes. Quaker history is full of painful paradoxes. A sketch of its general trends will illustrate these general observations.[1]

This chapter's foray into Quaker history may seem like a major digression from the book's stated concern for a sustainable life. But as we noted in Chapter 2, part of the vocation of a prophetic people is to see their present struggles in the perspective of their larger history. Within that perspective, it becomes impossible simply to write off one Quaker trend or branch as "wrong," or as "not Quaker." This chapter views the various renewals among Friends as a continuing effort to rebalance our Quaker faith and practice, and to *sustain its integrity* within the changing social ecology of its environment. The evolution of Friends over time, as they have migrated around the world and into various social habitats, has affinities with the changes natural species undergo in their spread to different environments. As we have suggested at different points in this book, ultimately the natural and spiritual are a single process of life on earth. We are made in the image of both God and the universe.

An Overview of Quaker History

Apocalyptic, Revolutionary Beginnings

The Quaker movement emerged as a recognizable phenomenon in the North of England in 1652. As suggested in Chapter 2, it was a prophetic outbreak that drew together a variety of religious and political radicals in an experiential, socially engaged movement, which grew exponentially in its first four years and sustained rapid growth for two decades. It was *apocalyptic* in the sense that it proclaimed the coming of Christ by means of the light's revelation in each person's conscience. The light had power to transform individuals and to gather communities that could challenge and overturn an unjust and violent society. Early Quaker preaching and ethical practice thus enacted the end of the world, a rupture in the normal state of human affairs.

It was a *revolutionary* movement: early Friends were willing to suffer and even die in resisting the oppressive order of their day, to testify to the power of Christ's light to transform their own lives, to transform the world, to spread the kingdom of heaven on earth, and to renew the creation. Their witness was consistently nonviolent but highly conflictual, as they vigorously confronted the religious establishment and an unjust social order.

Early Friends truly frightened the Puritan government of the 1650s and the restored monarchy after 1660. Until they were finally tolerated in 1689, more than four hundred and fifty Friends died under persecution in England and Wales. Thousands more survived harsh imprisonments. Fines against Friends totaled tens of thousands of pounds — a staggering amount in that day. This was clearly not an effort merely to found another religious denomination. Friends suffered for far more than the right to believe and worship as they preferred.[2]

But even by 1666, it was clear to Quaker leaders that the kingdom of heaven had been turned back by an alienated human society, by a nation on the threshold of imperial glory. They had not been "wrong" about the end of the world. But an alienated human society violently refuses to enter that reality. It flees the light's revelation.[3] Their revolution had been repressed and re-contained. Friends began to reposition themselves from a grassroots revolutionary movement to a hedged sect.

In the preceding chapter, we noted that the fuller organization of the early Quaker movement, including the introduction of formal roles of eldership, was controversial among the first generation of Friends. It produced a small but painful schism. The

Wilkinson-Story Separation of the 1670s was a reaction not only to the introduction of women and men elders. The standardization of Quaker organization into men's and women's monthly, quarterly, and yearly meetings offended others. The centralization of administration in the Second Day Meeting of Ministers, the Meeting for Sufferings, and staffed offices in London were a far cry from the loose, rapidly evolving network of the 1650s. George Fox, Margaret Fell, William Penn, and Robert Barclay were formidable leaders in this new phase of Quaker faith and practice. But these were shocking developments for those who wished to remain part of a more charismatic, freeform movement. Some also preferred less overt female leadership. Still, most Friends recognized that organization and leadership were necessary to a movement with a long-term future. A stable vessel was required to sustain the radical, prophetic spirituality, and countercultural social practices Friends had developed in the initial phase.

"Quietism," Orthopraxis

By the end of the seventeenth century, Friends had entered what is often called a "quietist" period. The term is misleading, however. Friends drew their sectarian boundaries distinctly against the cultural mainstream, but they were also highly innovative and successful in the world: in business, banking, science, and technology. In addition, they either governed or were highly influential in four American colonies. But over time, growing wealth, social accommodation, and political power also tended to compromise Quaker countercultural witness. By the middle of the eighteenth century, a coalition of concerned ministers and elders on both sides of the Atlantic called for a more radical faithfulness. The definitions and discipline of Quaker faith and practice were tightened over the second half of the century. The work of John Woolman, Anthony Benezet, and others in leading American Friends to renounce slaveholding was one facet of that larger reformation. But other lifestyle issues of dress, personal luxury, and demeanor also came under scrutiny.

This new astringency produced many disownments of Friends who would not conform. But it had other, admirable accomplishments.

For example, Friends in the colonial government of Pennsylvania withdrew from leadership rather than raise taxes to support the British government in the French and Indian War. Friends shifted their political energies to become more stalwart allies and advocates for Native American groups and for the abolition of slavery. Meanwhile, Quakers on both sides of the Atlantic also worked quietly to mediate the growing rift between Britain and the American colonies without resort to war. Their efforts were, of course, preempted by violent instigators on the American side. Accused as "loyalists," American Quakers became pariahs during the Revolution and the War of 1812. Their pacifism, abolitionism, and other countercultural testimonies (together with withering rates of disownment in some yearly meetings) transformed the Religious Society of Friends, the third largest American religious group in 1750, into a small, marginal, and sometimes despised sect.[4]

The quietist period, from the late seventeenth century into the early nineteenth century, is the classic period of Quaker faith and practice. Friends' internal order and behavioral codes were the most coherent and the most distinct from their surroundings of any time in Quaker history. It was the period of most highly developed *orthopraxis*, that is, right order and action. In this period elders, with responsibility for the right ordering of meetings and the moral standards of their members, were most influential.

But in a highly nuanced and paradoxical spirituality such as Quaker faith and practice, the maturity of such a trend eventually produces its contradiction and undoing. Over time, the dominance of eldership tended to intimidate vocal ministry in meetings. Even recorded ministers feared that elders would hear "the creature" (human thought and emotion), and not the pure leadings of the Spirit, speaking through their words. As a result, worship in some meetings felt less silent than silenced. As a result, the *faith* that informed their *practice* became increasingly implicit.

Doctrinal Renewal, Controversy, and Schism: Orthodoxy

Some Friends on both sides of the Atlantic found the doctrinal clarity of Wesleyan Methodism attractive. Moreover, Methodists were active in social reform, education, relief of the poor, abolition of slavery, and other causes resonant with Quaker testimony. They also held vibrant revivals and worship services that emphasized the movement of the Spirit among them, echoing in some respects the spiritual fervor of early Friends. Explicit Christian convictions were a strong motivating force behind these admirable traits. So some Friends began to adopt a more Wesleyan theology. In a relative vacuum of Quaker teaching, the differences between Wesleyan and Quaker theologies were either not apparent or seemed trivial to many. In the United States, westward migration also dislocated Friends from their traditional communities, inducing an amnesia of both faith and practice.

By 1800 fissures were appearing in the foundations of the Religious Society of Friends. After 1810, an Orthodox movement emerged among American yearly meetings, influenced by evangelical Wesleyan preaching. Elias Hicks, a traditionalist minister from Long Island, New York, became the most vocal critic of the new orthodoxy. He became the *cause celebre* for other traditional Friends who worried about mixing Quakerism with evangelical doctrine. Some of those who gathered around Hicks were not traditionalists but were attracted to Unitarianism and other early liberal trends. Their affinities in that direction were motivated by the same progressive social concerns that had drawn Orthodox Friends toward evangelicalism. But both Orthodox and Hicksite Friends were often oblivious to the differences between traditional Quaker faith and the diverging doctrines of evangelicals and Unitarians.

These two draws upon Quaker faith and practice are not surprising, especially when we consider that the early Quaker movement had emerged at the cusp of transition between the end of the Protestant Reformation and the beginnings of the liberal Enlightenment. Although traditional Quaker faith and practice is neither Protestant nor liberal, it is easy to mistake it either for an acute, ultimate form of Protestant Christianity, or for a proto-liberal expression of something more "rational." Friends holding one of these two perspectives are often scandalized by the other's approach. Together, they partake of the two great watersheds of Anglo-American culture that generate culture wars down to this day.

In the 1820s, controversy boiled over into outright separations in American yearly meetings. (A Beaconite controversy among British Friends produced a small schism along similar lines.) In the preceding chapter, we noted how the recorded minister Edward Hicks (cousin of Elias) struggled with anger during the throes of controversy and separation. Another Quaker minister, Joseph Hoag, reported that he lost his gift of discerning spiritual "conditions" among Friends during this same period. Thus, the static of conflict and polarization clouded the finer registers of Quaker spirituality, adding to the confusion and religious amnesia.

Ironically, the majority of Friends at the time of the separations were still traditionalists. Often it was the wealthier or more educated Friends who generated controversy and schism. Traditionalists were rarely bold or articulate enough to answer the evangelical and liberal innovators in their meetings. All parties believed they were upholding "true" Quaker faith and practice, and republished early Quaker writings to prove their case. The Orthodox branch was more explicitly interested in doctrine. But the more liberal elements in the Hicksite branch were developing an implicit counter-orthodoxy, based on principles of the goodness of human nature, the reliability of reason, and a faith in steady human progress. However, these principles were as extrinsic to traditional Quaker faith as was Methodist atonement theology.[5]

Thus, nineteenth-century Quaker history is best understood as a period in which concerns about belief (orthodoxy) became dominant and overturned the emphasis on behavior (orthopraxis). This trend was most dramatic in the Orthodox branch, where both theology and practices were rapidly transformed according to evangelical logic. Revival preaching and hymn singing were introduced among some before the Civil War. Pastoral leadership and programmed meetings for worship followed soon after the war. These were wholesale revisions of Quaker practice. Hicksites retained traditional forms of worship but, especially after 1870, their theology liberalized rapidly.

Meanwhile, both branches abandoned traditional norms of Quaker dress and lifestyle. Individual Friends were at liberty to adopt and adapt the traditional Quaker testimony of plainness as they felt led. Home visits from elders, who posed awkward questions about personal morality and lifestyle, were phased out. Congruent to the orthodox emphasis of this period, recognized ministers such as Elias Hicks, Joseph John Gurney, Lucretia Mott, and others were the key agents of change.[6]

Abiding Quaker traditionalists drew back from these trends in a series of separations beginning with the Wilburite controversy in the 1840s and continuing through the rest of the century. Most of these separations were from the Orthodox yearly meetings. Wilburite, or Conservative, yearly meetings were more determined and successful in maintaining the historic faith and practice of Friends. But based mainly in rural America, they slowly declined in numbers during the twentieth century. Despite miniscule numbers, the Christian faith and traditional practices of Conservative Friends still pose a trenchant counter-example to both evangelical and liberal Friends today. On the Hicksite side, a movement of Progressive Friends separated in the mid-nineteenth century, abandoning traditionalists to follow "new light" in several directions.

To return to the perspectives offered at the beginning of this chapter, both Orthodox and Hicksite Friends revised traditional Quaker faith and practice more profoundly than they realized. Those who defended more traditional ways couldn't make a convincing case to the innovators. The deeply prophetic Christian genius of Quaker faith and practice was largely lost. It became opaque and oddly quaint to most Friends as the nineteenth century progressed. The loss is tragic. But the new horizons opening before these diverging renewals elicited great energies of reform, evangelism, mission, and service. Quakers combined with other evangelicals in a variety of progressive social causes in the early to mid-nineteenth century. The Orthodox stream, particularly the more evangelical "Gurneyite" branch, grew dramatically in the latter nineteenth century. Traditional Quaker emphasis upon the light's perfecting power hybridized creatively with the evangelical "holiness" movement.[7]

But the wider evangelical movement in America turned more socially conservative during the latter nineteenth century in reaction to the American Civil War, the harsh new conditions of industrial life, and the social blights of American cities. Evangelical Friends, who increasingly took their cues from the wider evangelical and holiness movements, followed this more socially conservative trend. Evangelical Quaker renewal peaked in numbers and influence in the early twentieth century. As rural and small-town America has declined economically and depopulated over the past century, pastoral meetings have generally declined as well. They have not competed successfully with the evangelical churches they came to emulate so closely. However, early twentieth-century missionary ventures into East Africa and Latin America have been spectacularly successful.

Hicksite Friends slowly declined in numbers during the nineteenth century. But they collaborated with more liberal activists in the Orthodox yearly meetings to work for a variety of social reforms such as women's rights, the abolition of slavery, and the education of freed slaves. By the beginning of the twentieth century, in response to the catastrophic dimensions of modern warfare, they focused increasingly on international peacemaking.

Both evangelical and liberal renewals were important, recombinant forms of Quaker faith and practice. Friends had come out from sectarian seclusion and found new alliances (albeit in different directions) for spiritual renewal and social reconstruction. The more subtle resonances of Quaker faith and practice were not so much discarded as drowned out by the din of a wider culture awash with competing voices, amplified by new technologies of printing and distribution.

Progress and Process: Modern and Postmodern Renewals

But these developments, too, came to their moment of contradiction and undoing. After a century of doctrinal and counterdoctrinal developments, a modernist renewal returned to the early Quaker emphasis upon the authority of personal *experience*. George Fox's challenge, "What canst thou say?" echoed with new meaning, as Friends in Britain and America dropped doctrinal controversy to reconsider their actual spiritual experience in the context of a rapidly changing world. Modernist Friends considered their experience in light of the new findings of modern psychology. They championed the new, historically critical methods of biblical inter-pretation and re-read the Bible as a historical document rather than a doctrinal source-book. They began to affirm that Christianity contains truths in common with other great religions and partakes of a mysticism that forms the core of all true religion. They also embraced an evolutionary faith that human consciousness and the human condition are advancing through the centuries, enlight-ened by progressively higher revelations of truth, empowered by modern science and technology.

As this brief description suggests, modernist Friends reframed traditional Quaker emphasis upon unmediated religious expe-rience with a number of modern assumptions: psychology, evolutionary theory, confidence in scientific progress, and a his-torical perspective on the Bible. These new frames were largely attributable to increasing rates of higher education among Friends. They engaged Quaker faith and practice with a rapidly changing world. But modernist Friends often underestimated how differently they understood their experience, compared with the understand-ing of early and traditional Friends.

Interestingly, key leadership in the liberal-modernist renewal came not from the Hicksite yearly meetings, but from the liberal wing of the Orthodox branch. For example, Rufus Jones, a Gurneyite Friend from Maine, was its chief spokesperson, defining Quakerism as a mystical religion. Clarence Pickett, a one-time Friends pastor from Kansas, led the American Friends Service Committee through some of its classic phases in the 1930s and 1940s. Thomas Kelly, a product of Midwestern pastoral Quakerism, was a gifted exponent of modern spiritual disciplines. These and other key leaders were drawn away from the Gurneyite tradition toward more liberal ideals of Quaker faith and practice. It appears that the Hicksite tradition was less productive of leaders with a strong sense of calling to sus-tained, sacrificial service among Friends.

The numerical outreach of liberal-modernist renewal in Britain and America was not as dramatic as that of evangelical Friends in nineteenth-century America. But its social influence was consid-erable in the first half of the twentieth century. Rufus Jones and

Thomas Kelly were widely read in the liberal Christian mainstream. Many pacifists and social activists joined Friends, leaving other churches that were less hospitable to their convictions. The American Friends Service Committee and Friends Service Council (British) were path-breaking agents of Quaker concern for relief, reform, and social reconstruction. Representatives of these two organizations accepted the Nobel Peace Prize in 1947 following their relief and reconstruction work in Europe and Asia.

More shakeups were in store, however. The effect of two world wars, the introduction of nuclear warfare, and other sobering developments in modern science and technology dampened modernist confidence in progress after 1950. Meanwhile, the continuing secularization of British and American societies, together with interfaith exploration in a post-colonial world, shifted emphasis among liberal Friends from Christianity as a primary frame of reference toward a more truly universalist vision of Quaker faith and practice. The women's movement renewed the traditional feminist sensibilities of Friends. These latter twentieth-century developments deconstructed the Christocentric, Eurocentric, and androcentric frames within which the liberal sense of progress had hitherto been reckoned.

Liberal-modernist Quaker confidence in progress was thus eclipsed by a post-liberal, post-modern reliance upon *process*. Truth must be explored (if not ultimately defined) according to the respectful interaction of multiple perspectives. Thus, we find the modernist, mystical emphasis upon personal experience qualified by a growing concern for appropriate group processes to define provisional, working definitions of "our" truth. This shift amounts to a return to the orthopraxis of the "quietist" period, albeit on very different philosophical grounds. In this period, clerkship has become the form of leadership that is most prized and influential.[8]

Reflections

The historic shifts in Quaker faith and practice traced in this chapter may be charted thus:

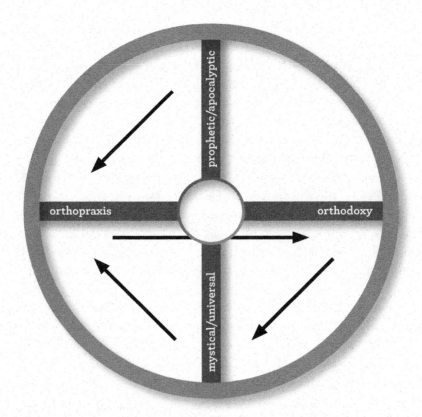

Here the horizontal axis denotes the interplay of orthopraxis (right practice) and orthodoxy (right belief). Quaker faith and practice amounts to this dialectic of belief and action, as they continually inform and redefine one another. Both are essential elements of Quaker life and witness. Different individuals and groups of Friends will place the emphasis differently. And we have seen how the emphasis shifted among Friends generally from the strong orthopractic thrust of the eighteenth century to the renewed concern for orthodoxy in the nineteenth century. Hicksites in America and liberal reformers in Britain shunned words like "doctrine" or "orthodoxy," but embraced a set of key convictions with the same passion that Orthodox and evangelical Friends upheld more traditional Christian doctrines.

Meanwhile, the vertical axis denotes the *mode* within which Friends experience and enact Quaker faith and practice, both orthodoxy and orthopraxis. Accordingly, the adjectives are more suggestive. Quaker faith and practice were first generated by early Friends experiencing and enacting the light in a *prophetic/apocalyptic* mode. This acutely biblical sensibility has a strong transcendent orientation. Even though the light is in each person's conscience, it is a light from *beyond* our best reckoning. Therefore, it is called an *inward* light; it shines within Friends, though originating from a greater source. The prophetic call of the light is to denounce injustice and violence in every social order and to announce the good news of the kingdom of heaven emerging among us. The light's revelation is apocalyptic in that it removes the veil from human, socially conceived reality. It thus demystifies human hierarchies and conventions. It reveals both our common humanity and our common destiny with all creation. The universe is viewed as the primal and ongoing work of a transcendent God, whose wisdom pervades all things. The inward light reveals that wisdom and repatterns our lives accordingly. The historical Jesus – inseparable from the inward, living Christ, the light personified – draws us into that divine destiny.

At the other pole, the modernist renewal of Quaker faith and practice enacts the *mystical/universal* mode. Here the orientation is more toward *immanence*, the nearness – even the sameness – between the light and the deepest, most authentic nature of our humanity. Rufus Jones, in his mystical reinterpretation of Quaker faith and practice, describes the divine as "unsundered" from the core of human nature. Thus, he writes of the *inner* light. Emphasis upon the union of divine and human heightens emphasis upon the light as *universal*, common to all human experience. The particularities of the biblical-Christian revelation are held more loosely, if at all. The vocational sense of a called people of God is likewise muted in favor of common cause with all peoples. The universe is more likely viewed as natural, rather than the creation of an all-transcending God. The divine wisdom in the universe is more often framed in terms of pantheism (everything is God), panentheism (God is in everything), or nontheism.

The twin modes of the prophetic/apocalyptic and the mystical/universal should not be turned into a dualism, any more than should orthopraxis and orthodoxy. Early Quakers can be viewed as mystics. Among early leaders, Isaac Penington probably comes closest to fitting that description. And George Fox strongly affirmed the universal presence and power of the light among all peoples, beyond the bounds of Christendom. He tested that conviction in conversations with Native Americans during his travels in America (1671-73). Likewise, there are strongly prophetic aspects in modern Quaker witness for peace and justice, even if the prophetic sense of calling and peoplehood is muted. Finally, both the prophetic/apocalyptic and the mystical/universal modes combine the personal with the collective, albeit in different ways. The former focuses them through a sense of being a people with a calling to universal service and mission, while the latter sustains a more diffuse but inclusive sense of common humanity.

Hence, Quaker faith and practice doesn't offer easy choices between orthopraxis versus orthodoxy, or prophetic Christian *versus* mystical universalist. Our integrity lies in the difficult, sometimes painful paradoxes we experience living in the middle of that powerful force field. Each new phase of Quaker history has been an attempt to rebalance the shifting energies of our faith and practice, while discovering new horizons of mission and service in the world.

Leadership and Differentiation

In the preceding chapter we suggested that the unity sought in the meeting's group discernment processes must be nurtured by various kinds of leaders. This differentiation-in-unity is organic to both the individual physical body's development and to the collective spiritual body of a local Friends meeting. Yet we have also found in this chapter that differentiation may foster diverging visions and callings that divide the collective body. Friends are therefore somewhat ambivalent about leadership. Leaders can unite, renew, and refocus the body. They can also divide it in the very process of renewal.

For example, the reforming ministers of the latter eighteenth century, including John Woolman, sought to shore up the behavioral boundaries of Friends. But the process led to the disownment of so many nonconforming Friends, we might well consider it an informal schism. Elias Hicks sought to defend the traditional unity of Quaker faith and practice, but became a lightning rod for the largest separation in Quaker history. Rufus Jones's efforts to modernize the Religious Society of Friends were met with resistance and schism in the Five Years Meeting of Gurneyite Friends.

When differentiation reaches the point of division, it becomes necessary to shift the comparison from the individual physical body to a population of a given species. As the population shifts locations to fill available ecological niches, it falls into subgroups that continue reproducing among themselves and may produce new varieties that diverge more strongly. By analogy, rapid westward migration was a major engine of change among American Friends in the nineteenth century. In the twentieth century differences between a rural and small-town social ecology versus that of cities and campuses has produced further changes. The two different environments continue to inspire profoundly divergent Quaker faiths and practices.

But Quaker faith and practice is more than the product of its environment, and the light is something beyond even our best selves. So how will Friends find renewal as the twenty-first century continues to unfold? Renewal has occurred and can occur again among Friends through the interaction of *three forms of transcendence*.

First, renewal requires recognized and emerging *leaders who are willing to transcend themselves*, to consecrate their lives, sacrifice middle-class privileges, and give themselves to work that not only advocates but models a prophetic faith. Second, that kind of commitment is nurtured by *a living relationship with a transcendent God/divinity* whose thoughts are not our thoughts (Isa. 55:8) and whose wisdom confounds our best reckoning (1 Cor. 1:18–25). And third, any authentic renewal must be *socially and species transcendent*. The Religious Society of Friends, at least in North America and Britain, is firmly embedded in a white, middle-class frame of reference and in unsustainable habits of consumption. Only the first and second forms of transcendence can jar us loose from this "parlor" of self-referential conversation over tea and cake.

As financial contractions and higher energy costs continue in the years ahead, Friends will become more rooted in a sense of *place*. The past century of expanding telecommunications and travel has helped us think more globally. The coming century may help us act more locally, responding to the poor in our communities, defending natural areas and struggling species, promoting more sustainable policies in local government. Paradoxically, our Friendship may become more truly universal as we become more grounded in the particularities of place.

Advices and Queries from Britain Yearly Meeting's *Quaker Faith & Practice*

#16: Do you welcome the diversity of culture, language and expressions of faith in our yearly meeting and in the world community of Friends? Seek to increase your understanding and to gain from this rich heritage and wide range of spiritual insights. Uphold your own and other yearly meetings in your prayers.

#17: Do you respect that of God in everyone though it may be expressed in unfamiliar ways or be difficult to discern? Each of us has a particular experience of God and each must find the way to be true to it. When words are strange or disturbing to you, try to sense where they come from and what has nourished the lives of others. Listen patiently and seek the truth which other people's opinions may contain for you. Avoid hurtful criticism and provocative language. Do not allow the strength of your convictions to betray you into making statements or allegations that are unfair or untrue. Think it possible that you may be mistaken.

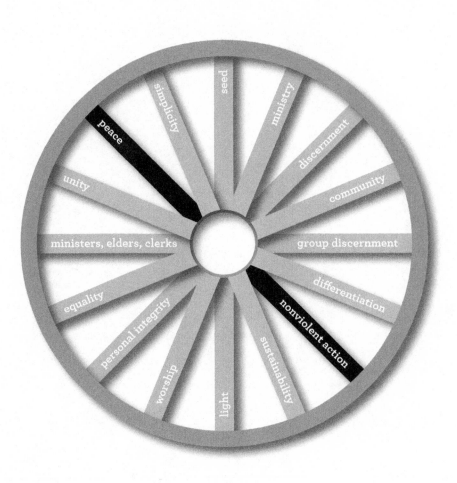

CHAPTER 7

The Lamb's War

As we have seen repeatedly in these chapters, Quaker faith and practice are energized by a pattern of powerful paradoxes. Peace is no exception. On one hand, there is the sublime peace, a vitalizing harmony that attends our quiet abiding in the divine Presence, as God teaches and heals us through every cell of our bodies. Recall again (from Chapter 2) the counsel of George Fox:

> *The first step of peace is to stand still in the light (which discovers things contrary to it) for power and strength to stand against that nature which the light discovers: for here grace grows, here is God alone glorified and exalted, and the unknown truth, unknown to the world, made manifest, which draws up that which lies in prison and refresheth it in time, up to God, out of time, through time.*[1]

Note, however, that "the first step of peace" leads to conflict. First we "stand still" in the light. Then the light reveals things in our lives contrary to its nature. Then the light gives us strength to "stand against" desires, habits and personal investments that are in conflict with the light's nature – and with our own true nature in the seed of God. Any peace that simply denies or glosses over such conflict is a false peace, what the prophet Isaiah (28:17–18) calls a "refuge of lies," a "covenant with death."[2]

Hence, true peace is the hidden sanctuary of individuals and communities willing to face conflict, endure struggle, and choose life over death, As Fox's counsel suggests, it is a struggle for liberation from captivity to sin and delusion. The liberation is both personal and social. It takes us "up to God, out of time," but only "in time, through time." *This peace is not the absence of conflict.* It is the integrative, covenantal reality implied by the Hebrew word *shalom*: wholeness, communion; a harmonious equilibrium that balances needs and claims among all parties; an intact, orderly rightness of life.[3]

The sustainable life will not be found through a narrow focus on personal habits of consumption or environmental advocacy, to the neglect of work for justice and struggle against militarism, or attention to the life of our meetings. Friends are sometimes at odds over which of these concerns deserves our most urgent attention. Different Friends will prioritize different concerns, often based on their different gifts and abilities. But all these concerns make some claim on us, and hopefully any given meeting community will balance these different emphases among its participants. The integrative *shalom* of true peace is the product of covenant communities.

The Lamb's War

Early Friends named this paradoxical reality "the Lamb's War." It begins within, as one stands still in the light, sees what must change, and begins to follow Christ out of captivity and into freedom. It builds powerful bonds of love and mutual support among those struggling to be faithful in the light together. Individuals not only support one another through personal struggles; they also inspire each other by example and gentle encouragement to a higher attainment. The Lamb's War thus moves outward to form and continually reform a community of equals.

The covenantal community sees the world around it with new eyes. Social norms and mores that once appeared "natural," self-evident, or simply unfortunate are revealed in the light to be intolerable travesties of human decency and of God's good will to all creation. The Lamb's War is an engagement with norms and institutions that oppress and violate God's creatures. It is a struggle against spiritual forces that keep men and women locked in alienation from the knowledge and power of God within them. The term "Lamb's War" derives from Revelation 14:1-5, in which John sees Christ as a lamb standing on Mount Zion (the spiritual mountain Micah saw — see

Chapter 4) with faithful men and women standing together with the lamb. They stand against the violent and alienating powers of the Beast and False Prophet (portrayed in Rev. 13). The early Quaker Lamb's War confronted a variety of social injustices. But it focused primarily against the established Church of England with its monopoly on religion, its power to coerce all to attend, its vast properties, and its enfranchised clergy supported by state-enforced tithes. Early Friends by the thousands nonviolently confronted the state-church alliance that deformed human consciousness by forcing it to conform to creeds and swear oaths of allegiance.

Over the centuries since that first generation, the experience of peace has led Friends into conflict with a variety of social monstrosities. For example, for John Woolman and Levi Coffin (a leader in the Underground Railroad), the pre-eminent monstrosity was the institution of slavery. For Lucretia Mott and Susan B. Anthony, slavery was compounded by patriarchy. For twentieth-century Friends, it has been the massively enfranchised military-industrial complex.

Early Friends began in the North but had soon infiltrated every parish in England, interrupting church services and challenging the authority of the state-enfranchised clergy. They were often attacked by mobs, taken before judges, and thrown in prison. Benjamin Nicholson and two other Quakers imprisoned at York castle published *The Three-Fold Estate of Anti-Christ* (1653), portraying the clergy, legal establishment, and ruling classes as an unholy trinity united against the risen Christ moving among the common people. The same year, Nicholson published *A Blast from the Lord*, inveighing against the social arrogance and wealth of magistrates and others who

> *spend the creatures on your lusts, in glorious apparels, and gold rings, and needless adorning, instead of covering the naked, and feeding the hungry, you set out Laws to punish them: my heart bleeds to think of the hard usage of my poor fellow creatures that have no abiding. . . . You wallow yourselves in the earths treasure like swine in the mire, and never consider that the earth is the Lords and the fullness thereof, and that he hath given it to the sons of men in general, not to*

a few lofty ones which Lord it over their brethren: and if any poor creature steal a horse, ox, or sheep, he is either put to death, or burned in the hand; but you never consider how many horses, oxen, and sheep you steal from the Lord and use them to satisfy your own wills and lusts.[4]

John Camm wrote *A Word of the Lord* to Oliver Cromwell in 1654, making the case for disestablishment of the church: "we witness the coming of Christ in his Kingdom, not by might, pomp, glory from without, nor any law . . . our desires were that there should be no Law upon Religion, for it need not one to defend it, for pure religion . . . is to loose the bonds of wickedness, and let the oppressed go free, and take off every yoke."[5]

The early Quaker Lamb's War was grounded not only in the deep spiritual baptism of standing still in the light and becoming whole persons — it also derived from the bitter lessons of the English Civil War in the previous decade, which had only succeeded in enfranchising a new set of oppressive elites. George Fox diagnosed the spiritual malaise underlying violence and war. In April 1651, while serving a sentence in Derby for blasphemy, the Parliamentary army tried to recruit him to fight against a royalist uprising:

My time being nearly out of being committed six months to the House of Correction, they filled the House of Correction with persons that they had taken up to be soldiers: and then they would have me to be a captain of them to go forth to Worcester [to] fight and the soldiers cried they would have none but me. So . . . the Commissioners . . . proferred me that preferment because of my virtue, as they said, with many other compliments, and asked me if I would not take up arms for the Commonwealth against the King. But I told them I lived in the virtue of that life and power that took away the occasion of all wars, and I knew from whence all wars did rise, from the lust according to James's doctrine [James 4:1]. Still they courted me to accept of their offer and thought that I did but compliment with them. But I told them I was come into the covenant of peace which was before wars and strifes were.

And they said they offered it in love and kindness to me because of my virtue, and such like flattering words they used, and I told them if that were their love and kindness I trampled it under my feet. Then their rage got up and they said, "Take him away gaoler, and cast him into the dungeon amongst the rogues and felons"; which they did and put me into the dungeon amongst thirty felons in a lousy, stinking low place in the ground without any bed. Here they kept me a close prisoner almost a year.[6]

Fox's life in the light, the covenant of peace, had given him insight into the real motives of the Civil War and of all wars, the lust for property and power (excoriated by Nicholson above). Although his political sympathies were decidedly with the Commonwealth, he refused to join its battles, which would only harden power into oppression.

Just a year later, having sparked an explosive Quaker movement in the North, Fox stated the peace principle in positive — but still highly conflictual — terms in an epistle to Friends:

That which is set up by the sword, is held up by the sword; and that which is set up by spiritual weapons is held up by spiritual weapons, and not by carnal weapons. The peace-maker hath the Kingdom, and is in it; and hath the dominion over the peace-breaker, to calm him in the power of the Lord. And Friends, let the waves [persecution] break over your heads. There is rising a new and living way out of the north, which makes the nations like waters [Rev. 17:15]. The days of virtue, love and peace are come and coming, and the Lamb had and hath the kings of the earth to war withal [i.e., against — see Rev. 17:14] and will overcome with the sword of the Spirit, and the word of his mouth [Rev. 19:21].[7]

As the citations in this passage indicate, the Book of Revelation was a major source for early Friends. Its message of prophetic resistance to oppressive, idolatrous power helped shape a nonviolent movement that included many men who had fought valiantly for the Commonwealth in the preceding decade. Their confrontational witness enraged their opponents more often than they calmed them. They were physically attacked or thrown in prison. But their lions-den strategy drew out sympathetic spirits and brought them into the movement, which grew exponentially in these earliest, militant years.

The concept of spiritual weaponry was drawn from the Letter to the Ephesians (6:10-15), which calls early Christians to

> *be strong in the Lord and in the strength of his power. Put on the whole armor of God, so that you may be able to stand against the wiles of the devil. For our struggle is not against enemies of blood and flesh, but against the rulers, against the authorities, against the cosmic powers of this present darkness, against the spiritual forces of evil in the heavenly places. Therefore take up the whole armor of God, so that you may be able to withstand on that evil day, and having done everything, to stand firm. Stand therefore, and fasten the belt of truth around your waist, and put on the breastplate of righteousness. As shoes for your feet put on whatever will make you to proclaim the gospel of peace.*

Note the emphasis upon *standing*: "stand against," "withstand," "stand firm," and "stand." This language partakes of a nonviolent undercurrent in scripture going all the way back to the Exodus from Egypt. The Israelites despaired as they stood on the banks of the Red Sea, with Egyptian chariots bearing down on them from behind and deep waters ahead. "But Moses said to the people, 'Do not be afraid, stand firm, and see the deliverance that the Lord will accomplish for you today, for the Egyptians you see today you shall never see again. The Lord will fight for you, and you have only to keep still'" (Exod. 14:13-14).

So George Fox's counsel to "stand still in the light" is much more than spiritual technique. It is a path of personal transformation, nonviolent conflict, and social liberation. Alienated powers will do most of the moving. The faithful need simply to stand fast in the integrity, equality, community, simplicity, and peace they find together. Strength will be given. Words will be given as needed. Actions will be led where they are appropriate. Speaking truth to power, we stand with the Lamb, who "will overcome with the sword of the Spirit, and the word of his mouth."

Ephesians emphasizes that the struggle is not against "blood and flesh" people but against the spiritual forces that control them: "against the rulers, against the authorities, against the cosmic powers of this present darkness, against the spiritual forces of evil in the heavenly places." New Testament scholar Walter Wink interprets these "powers" as the spirituality, or interiority, of social institutions, structures, and systems. These powers are part of God's good creation, but have been disordered by forces of delusion and domination.[8] The work of redeemed humanity is to resist disordered powers and to call them back to their places in the many-faceted wisdom of God.

James Nayler was a leading figure in the early Quaker movement. While in prison in 1657, he wrote *The Lamb's War*, the definitive statement of the movement's revolutionary struggle. He summarizes the Quaker program:

> *Their war is not against Creatures, not with the flesh and blood but spiritual wickedness exalted in the hearts of Men and Women, against the whole Work and Device of the god of this World, Laws, Customs, Fashions, Inventions, this is all Enmity against the Lamb and his followers who are entered into the Covenant which was from the beginning. [The Lamb has come] to take the Government to himself that God alone may wholly rule in the hearts of Men and man live in the Work of God.[9]*

Nayler describes an all-embracing nonviolent cultural revolution. It aims to resist and transform all unjust, oppressive, and violent structures and norms. It wages conflict on behalf of a new order in which "God alone may wholly rule in the hearts of Men and man live in the Work of God." This is nothing less than a reconciliation of culture and nature, a redemption that brings human life back to earth, back in tune with the wisdom of creation.

Peace and Justice

The coordinates of the Lamb's war, and the Quaker practice of peace witness generally, may be charted thus:

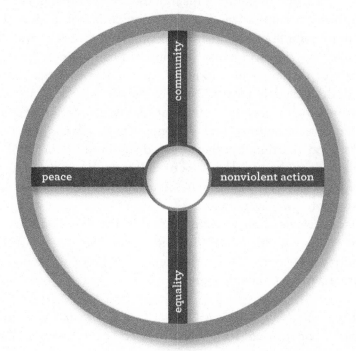

The experience of peace in personal spiritual practice and in Quaker worship builds an egalitarian community. Empathy grows for one another and for others in society in the consciousness *razing* experience of the light. That is, the light deconstructs and reconstructs the self and the world in one's conscience. One can no longer accept or justify society's violence and injustice as "the way the world works." Individuals and communities of Friends are led into prophetic confrontation and conflict with these deformed powers and with individuals who have been deformed by the powers.

The vertical axis of equality and community is like a plumb line in the consciousness of the community that gathers and follows the light together. Community experience tests and grounds our ideals of equality, winnowing out distorted ideas in some cases, challenging us to think and act more radically in other cases. Meanwhile, our commitment to equality among all kinds of people forces us to keep looking afresh at our community and asking whether it is sound. The prophet Amos waited upon the Lord and was given a vision of a plumb line set amid the people of Israel. It revealed the crookedness of a society that had abridged God's covenant, polarizing between rich and poor, powerful and powerless. Such an unsound edifice must fall (Amos 7:7-9). In a similar vein, Isaiah warned that the Lord "will make justice the line, and righteousness the plummet" in judging human society (28:17).

The horizontal axis of peace and nonviolent action is a continuum. Personal peace is found only through confronting and standing against one's inner contradictions. Coming more fully into the light, we help one another in that struggle, as fellow "children of the light." Together we take the struggle into wider society. But even in the heat of prophetic confrontation, it is possible to maintain inner peace, equanimity, and compassion. In 1652 George Fox was beaten half unconscious by a mob of Christians near Ulverston. But even in that moment "I was in the love of God to them all." After the beating, "they said if I came into the town again they would kill me. And so I was moved of the Lord to come up again through them."[10]

James Nayler was savagely punished by an act of Parliament in 1656. Still, at the end of his life he was able to witness:

> *There is a Spirit that I feel, which delights to do no Evil, nor to revenge any Wrong, but delights to endure all things, in Hope to enjoy its own in the end; its hope is to out-live all Wrath and Contention, and to weary out all Exaltation and Cruelty, or whatsoever is of Nature contrary to itself.*[11]

These two perpendicular axes constitute each other. The peace of Quaker faith and practice reveals social justice more starkly. Simultaneously, the unmasking of unjust, alienated social relations draws Friends into nonviolent engagement with oppressive, violent persons and powers. This dialectic, taken as a whole, is the meaning of *shalom*, a peace the world cannot give (John 14:17), a peace that surpasses all understanding (Phil. 4:7). Those who pose a choice between working for peace and working for justice don't really understand either.

On the other hand, when Friends simply react in protest to the next war, or simply refuse military service without addressing the exploitative economic system that gives rise to militarism and war, the Quaker "peace testimony" becomes one dimensional and something less than a full testimony to the truth. Furthermore, even to work for both peace and justice is a hollow exercise if we don't simplify our lives and minimize our participation in an economic system that oppresses others. In Chapter 4, we heard the sobering lament of John Woolman (1764):

> *Oh, that we who declare against wars and acknowledge our trust to be in God only, may walk in the Light and therein examine our foundation and motives in holding great estates! May we look upon our treasures and the furniture of our houses and the garments in which we array ourselves and try whether the seeds of war have any nourishment in these our possessions or not.*[12]

Hence, simplicity (the aspect of Quaker testimony we will address in the final chapter) is also implied in peace. Indeed, the aim of this book is to show how every aspect of Quaker faith and practice is implicit in every other. Each is integral to the whole, the "seamless garment" of the crucified and risen Christ. Thus, to lift up "peace" as the distinguishing mark of Friends, to the neglect of other integral aspects, is to reify ("thingify") one part of the whole and to reduce the powerful processes of faith and practice into a static "Quaker philosophy" and pristine "Quaker values."

The Declaration of 1661

The first definitive articulation of the Quaker commitment to peace came in an emergency statement published by Fox and a dozen Quaker leaders in London in January 1661. In the aftermath of an armed uprising in London by another radical group, several hundred Friends had been rounded up and imprisoned to ensure the security of the newly restored monarchy. *A Declaration from the harmless and innocent people of God, called Quakers, against all plotters and fighters in the world* was drafted and rushed into print to secure the release of imprisoned Friends and make the Quaker position clear to the new government. The document begins:

> *Our principle is, and our practices have always been, to seek peace and ensue it and to follow after righteousness and the knowledge of God, seeking the good and welfare and doing that which tends to the peace of all. We know that wars and fightings proceed from the lusts of men (as James 4:1-3), out of which lusts the Lord hath redeemed us, and so out of the occasion of war. The occasion of which war, and war itself (wherein envious men, who are lovers of themselves more than lovers of God, lust, kill and desire to have men's lives or estates) ariseth from lust. All bloody principles and practices we ... do utterly deny, with all outward wars and strife and fightings with outward weapons, for any end or under any pretence whatsoever. And this is our testimony to the whole world.*[13]

The spiritual struggle of the Lamb's war is not denied. The tract goes on to add, "our weapons are spiritual and not carnal, yet mighty through God to the plucking down of the strongholds of Satan, who is the author of wars, fighting, murder, and plots."[14] But the larger agenda of social justice and equality has been attenuated here, in order to emphasize a refusal to participate in violence.

The overall tract is a powerful statement, one of the great peace witnesses in all Christian history. But, with Friends increasingly under persecution from a hostile new regime, the larger social equation of peace was neglected. Friends suffered more than ever, but most often merely for continuing to meet openly for worship, rather than for preaching in the streets, marketplaces, and parish churches, calling people to justice and morality. "The Quaker peace testimony" as we know it came into focus only as the Lamb's War was defeated and Quakers were repressed to become a nonconformist sect, as described in the overview of Quaker history in the preceding chapter.

The Development of "the Quaker Peace Testimony"

William Penn's writings set the pattern for post-revolutionary, early modern Quaker faith and practice in several respects, including peace. His *Essay towards the Present and Future Peace of Europe* (1693) was a far-sighted proposal for a "Diet" of European states to settle international disputes and establish laws for international conduct. It retained the radical Quaker peaceable kingdom as its standpoint, but it suggested pragmatic ways to limit and de-escalate the protracted crisis of European warfare until that kingdom is realized. Penn pointed out that a different rule holds for "the people of God," which is "not fighting but suffering." But he knew that this was not an ethic rulers or the majority of Europeans were ready to accept. His proposals trenchantly prefigured today's International Court at the Hague and the European Union.[15]

Penn thus established the two-track logic of modern Quaker peacemaking. As *prophets*, Friends maintain the absolute renunciation of violence and are willing to suffer for their nonviolent witness for a peaceful and just world. As *reconcilers*, Friends also meet hostile parties and warring powers where they are and work to find pragmatic alternatives to resolving conflict among them. Different Friends typically have strengths along one track or the other, as radical prophets or negotiating reconcilers. The interplay of these different gifts and callings defines the creative edge of Quaker peacemaking to this day.

In the classic, so-called "quietist" period, the countercultural sectarian impetus of faith and practice led Friends primarily to an ethic of resistance to military service. Some, like John Woolman, also resisted payment of taxes for war. As noted in the preceding chapter, the renunciation of war led Friends to withdraw from colonial leadership in Pennsylvania during the French and Indian War. It also inspired concerted efforts by Friends on both sides of the Atlantic to avert the violence of the American Revolution. Friends also advocated for Native American tribes against the onslaught of European American aggression.

English Friend Jonathan Dymond's *Inquiry into the Accordancy of War with the Principles of Christianity* (1823)[16] is the first systematic expression of the Quaker peace testimony. It constitutes a pacifist correlate to the drive for doctrinal renewal emerging in the Orthodox and Hicksite movements at that same time. Dymond devotes half of his book to showing the incompatibility of war with

Christian faith. He stresses that pacifism is not only good Christianity but good sense. War is unreasonable and disastrous to human society. He asserts that peace is a practical policy for nations, but he doesn't develop institutional alternatives to war. Peter Brock cites Dymond's book as a seminal influence on the development of the international peace movement in the ensuing decades of the nineteenth century. It brought the Quaker peace testimony out of sectarian seclusion and contributed to wider Christian peace work.[17]

By the end of the nineteenth century, Friends on both sides of the Atlantic were on the forefront of religious and secular peace societies. A Friends peace conference in Philadelphia in 1900 rehearsed major themes of the century to come. Military-industrial establishments in Europe and America were already casting dark clouds over the future prospects of peace. The Spanish-American War had revealed imperialist tendencies in the United States extending beyond North America. Despite these forebodings, Rufus Jones, the emerging trans-Atlantic leader of liberal-modernist renewal (see the preceding chapter) breathed confidence in the inexorable progress of a Christian civilization. These, of course, were heady days of rapid scientific, technological, and economic advancement.

Two world wars and the rise of a permanent war economy in the United States made peace the perennially pressing concern among Friends. "The peace testimony" became the defining feature of "Quakerism" for many Friends. Peace became the lens through which Friends viewed all concerns. A good specimen statement is found in Britain Yearly Meeting's *Quaker Faith & Practice*:

> *The Peace Testimony has been a source of inspiration to Friends through the centuries, for it points to a way of life which embraces all human relationships. . . . In the closing years of the twentieth century, we as Friends face a bewildering array of social and international challenges, which have widened the relevance of the Peace Testimony from the issue of peace and war between states to problems of tensions and conflicts in all their forms.[18]*

Concern for peace has indeed exerted a powerful shaping influence on Quaker witness regarding race relations, civil rights, economic justice, women's rights, prison reform, international development, interfaith dialogue, earth care, and just about every other area of social action among Friends.

In the preceding chapter, we noted that during the latter twentieth century, the modern Quaker confidence in progress, reckoned from a Christian-European-masculine perspective, was transfigured to become a postmodern faith in processes that foster a shared search for truth among different religious, racial, and gendered perspectives. This perspective offers a healthy critique of all false unities that obliquely establish the dominance of one viewpoint or interest above others. But it also tends to establish a permanent, uneasy rivalry between racial, gender, sexual, religious, and other identities that are never resolved. These jostling identities have tended to enervate the Religious Society of Friends today, weakening wider efforts in outreach and witness.

By contrast, early Friends were united and galvanized into revolutionary action by spiritual formation in *Christ*, whose historic example and spiritual presence through the light within each person's conscience is also *beyond* every personal identity. The living Christ also stands not only beyond every doctrinal formulation, but beyond every abstract ethical value such as "peace." Returning once again to Fox's counsel, "the first step of peace is to stand still in the light." Through that steadfast patience, "the unknown truth, unknown to the world, [is] made manifest, which draws up that which lies in prison and refresheth it in time, up to God, out of time, through time." This is the truth that makes us free (John 8:32). Peace and nonviolent action are the way of that freedom.

Advices and Queries from Britain Yearly Meeting's *Quaker Faith & Practice*

#31: We are called to live "in the virtue of that life and power that takes away the occasion of all wars." Do you faithfully maintain our testimony that war and the preparations for war are inconsistent with the spirit of Christ? Search out whatever in your own way of life may contain the seeds of war. Stand firm in our testimony, even when others commit or prepare to commit acts of violence, yet always remember that they too are children of God.

#32: Bring into God's light those emotions, attitudes and prejudices in yourself which lie at the root of destructive conflict, acknowledging your need for forgiveness and grace. In what ways are you involved in the work of reconciliation between individuals, groups and nations?

#33: Are you alert to practices here and throughout the world which discriminate against people on the basis of who or what they are or because of their beliefs? Bear witness to the humanity of all people, including those who break society's conventions or its laws. Try to discern new growing points in social and economic life. Seek to understand the causes of injustice, social unrest and fear. Are you working to bring about a just and compassionate society which allows everyone to develop their capacities and fosters the desire to serve?

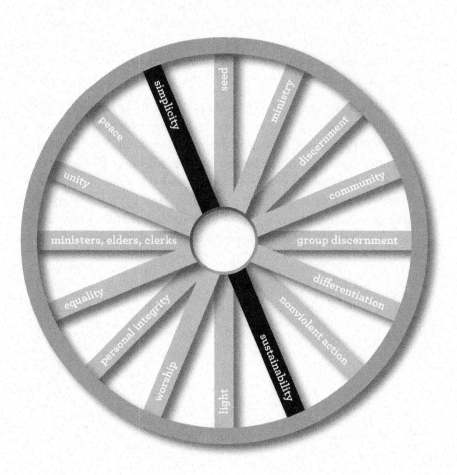

CHAPTER 8

Daily Delight

Some readers may be disappointed that we are only now in the final chapter really coming to the issue of "sustainability," as we usually conceive it: that is, the crisis of our life on this finite planet. But clearly, the material questions of pollution, population, and resource use have spiritual dimensions. Thus, we have needed to set deep foundations, starting with Quaker spiritual formation in daily practice, to grapple in a sustainable way with the issues of sustainability. From the holistic perspective we have been building chapter by chapter, "sustainability" becomes not just one more matter we're concerned about, not simply a new "testimony." Sustainability is a way of re-viewing the whole of Quaker practice, of integrating all the dynamic tensions we have contemplated along the way. The "groans of creation," a planet beset by our human folly (see Introduction) are one with our own groans in the Spirit, our longing for personal liberation, for a life in harmony with one another, for a life in balance with our planet. As suggested in the Introduction, the scope of or inquiry might be called "deep sustainability."

If peace was the dominant theme of Quaker testimony in the twentieth century, the interaction between personal simplicity and work for a sustainable human society on earth will focus much of our imagination and energies in this century. It has to. Anything less will amount to nihilism and massive destruction – a path we have traveled disastrously far already. Without the personal practice of simplicity, concern for sustainability becomes doctrinaire, "words without life," as early Friends would say. Conversely, without the global vision of a sustainable future, the personal practice of simplicity can easily become more a matter of style than substance. Twentieth-century Friend Mildred Binns Young preferred to speak of principled "poverty" rather than "simplicity" for that very reason.[1]

Early Friends found sources of earth-wisdom in the Hebrew and Christian Scriptures that helped them understand the light's inner teaching. We can gain valuable perspectives from those sources as well. In Chapter 3 we saw how Jesus's teaching in the Sermon on the Mount (Matt. 5-7) advocates a way of life that combines integrity, simplicity, peace, and community — what we often call "Quaker testimonies" — in an integrative whole. Much of the time, Jesus taught in the idioms of Jewish folk wisdom. The wisdom tradition is represented in Hebrew scripture by the books of Proverbs, Job, and Ecclesiastes, and in prophets such as Amos. The wisdom tradition emphasizes that divine wisdom can be learned from observing the patterns of nature, God's creation.

In Proverbs 8:22-36, wisdom (Hebrew *Hokma* or Greek *Sophia*) is portrayed as a feminine personality. She was there at the beginning of creation, working alongside God as a "master worker," collaborating with "daily delight." The patterns they planted in the natural world contain lessons for personal life and a just society. *Hokma* concludes, "And now my children, listen to me: happy are those who keep my ways. Hear instruction and be wise, and do not neglect it. Happy is the one who listens to me, watching daily at my gates, waiting beside my doors. For whoever finds me finds life and obtains favor from the Lord: but those who miss me injure themselves; all who hate me love death" (32-36). In a similar fashion, the Sermon on the Mount (Matt. 5:3-12) begins with Beatitudes that bless (the Greek *makarios* — "blessed" — can also be translated "happy") those whose attitudes and actions embody wisdom.[2]

During his short years of ministry Jesus gathered a movement that mixed religious people with common peasants, the destitute, and social outcasts of many kinds. He preached that "wisdom is justified by all her children" (Luke 7:35). So he invited both rich and poor, the respectable and the despised, into what he called "the kingdom of heaven" or "the kingdom of God," a realm that is not coming someday but is *already* "among/within you" (Luke 17:21). It is open to everyone. But it is subtle, difficult to recognize, and not always easy to enter. So Jesus utilized a variety of everyday agrarian parables and household metaphors to describe the kingdom. He compared it to seeds sprouting, harvests gathered, yeast spreading, and house cleaning. These similes and parables partake of the Hebrew-Jewish wisdom that finds the patterns for wise living and a just society through observing natural, everyday phenomena. The movement Jesus started among Galilean peasants, fishermen, and homemakers was a movement of people who lived close to the earth.

But Jesus was also an apocalyptic prophet. His use of the term "kingdom of heaven" provoked Jewish end time hopes that God would soon redeem Israel from Roman captivity. This prophetic aspect of Jesus's ministry came into sharper focus as he moved southward to Judea and confronted the Roman occupation more acutely. He saw his people struggling with it in three main ways. First, there was a conservative priestly-aristocratic class (Sadducees) who controlled the Jerusalem temple and collaborated with the Romans, both to enfranchise themselves but also to minimize Roman violence against their people. Second, there was a more middle-class movement of scribes and Pharisees. They hoped for liberation from the Romans. But in the meantime, they practiced an elaborate regimen of cultic rituals and moral codes. These were devised to maintain Jewish purity and integrity until the Messiah came to deliver the people. Third, there was a middle-to-lower-class movement of Zealots. These were bandits and revolutionaries often based in the hills, making guerrilla strikes here and there, while dreaming of a Messiah who would lead them in holy war to drive out the Romans and re-establish an independent Jewish kingdom, the kingdom of God.

Jesus saw his people on a collision course with the Roman Empire. He warned of this in dire, "end of the world" terms, especially during his last days in Jerusalem. Indeed, some forty years after Jesus's death, a Zealot-ignited revolt ended in the Roman destruction of the temple and most of Jerusalem. Many thousands of Jews were slaughtered or carried off into Roman slavery. It was a horrific "end of the world" as first-century Palestinian Jews knew it.

But until he was crucified by the Romans, Jesus was building some kind of fourth option. We can only guess what he intended and what was taking shape by the time of his death. The gospels focus the life of Jesus primarily in terms of his death and its meaning for the movement that succeeded him. But from his recorded teachings and anecdotal information about his followers, we can surmise some general features of the movement Jesus was building. In proclaiming a general amnesty (forgiveness) and inviting "the lost sheep of Israel" into the kingdom of heaven, he drew together all kinds of people to start over with God and with each other, to begin living a communal life of cooperation and mutual aid. It was a simple, subsistence life that built networks below the power structures of the day. Even during his lifetime, Jesus sent his disciples out to expand that informal network. This was the seed of some kind of nonviolent social revolution from below.

Jesus did not seek to overthrow Rome or the priestly collaborationist regime. Rather, it appears that he was building a grassroots Jewish society that could manage with or without them. He viewed the temple as "a den of robbers" sapping the religious energies and finances of the people. Moreover, he saw that the temple was doomed if conflict with the Romans boiled over into revolt. The violent Zealot option was morally wrong and tactically insane. Jesus taught an ethic of peaceful reconciliation among all kinds of people, together with nonviolent resistance to oppressive power. He drew many sympathizers from among the scribes and Pharisees. But their middle-class religious sensibilities were repeatedly offended by the company Jesus kept. For his part, Jesus felt that scribes had turned the laws of Moses into a fussy regimen that poor people didn't have the luxury to practice. He reminded Pharisees that the law was made for humans, not humans for the law (Mark 2:27).

By the time the New Testament gospels were written, the destruction of Jerusalem had taken place and the Jesus movement had been transfigured to become the Christian movement, an international, interclass, multicultural movement spreading rapidly around the eastern Mediterranean. The Palestinian Jewish movement Jesus himself had started was barely remembered as such. His violent death and his re-emergence at large through his Spirit reframed everything he had said and done in powerful new ways.

We noted something similar in the preceding chapter, in terms of the Quaker peace testimony. The Lamb's War of the 1650s had been a powerful, nonviolent, revolutionary movement. But after 1660 the revolutionary meaning of the movement was gradually lost, and "peace" was distilled out for future generations with a rather different meaning. By 1700 the original impetus of the first, revolutionary decade was forgotten even by Friends.[3]

Living in the End Times

So what is the point of all this for Quaker faith and practice today? The point is that we live in times that are similarly apocalyptic. "The end of the world" became scientifically plausible in the aftermath of two horrendously destructive world wars and the advent of nuclear weapons. Although we have pulled back from the brink of conflagration with the end of the Cold War, the threat of nuclear catastrophe still looms in various forms today.

But during the second half of the last century, "the end of the world" has become not just an imminent threat but *an unfolding tragedy*. Resource depletion, environmental degradation, population pressures, accelerating species extinctions, and climate change — combined with the ruthless exploitation of large sectors of humanity through global capitalist expansion and the chronic state of war required to maintain that system — are ending the world day by day. We who live in enclaves of wealth and privilege ignore this reality only through a denial as systematic and vehement as the system itself.

That stark reality has inspired this little book as an attempt to reframe all of our Quaker faith and practice in terms of sustainability. Sustainability is not just another plank in a Quaker political platform. And Quaker faith and practice is not a list dos and don'ts. It is an integrative whole, where each aspect informs and enlivens the others. This book has presented it as a set of paradoxes and energizing tensions. But all of these need to be contemplated within the horizon of a sustainable life on the earth. That is the compelling and pervasive reality of our world, the horizon within which the human race will henceforth live or die.

Our present systemic crisis inspires a set of responses similar to those of Jesus's day. First, we find a coalition of upper-class economic interests and right-wing religious groups collaborating with the global economic system and its enforcing military-industrial establishment. They capture the loyalty of large sectors of the population who are fearful for their own security and enthralled by the trappings of power and its religious justifications. Second, there are hard-working middle-class people, many of them religious, who may entertain moderate to liberal social values and are disturbed by the powers that have taken over their nation and the world. They have concern for the poor and the oppressed, but are uncomfortable mixing with them. They are concerned for "the environment" but find it difficult to renounce the material comforts and consumer items they have worked hard to attain. Finally, there are elements seething with resentment and violent desires to strike out at the system in whatever ways they can. These include fundamentalist elements in several different religions, sometimes organized into terrorist networks, but also individuals and groups who simply erupt with blind rage in violent outbursts at schools, theaters, and public events.

What would be a fourth option within the logic of our situation, like the one Jesus generated in his day? My vision is limited. But I believe it would, like the early Quaker movement, combine an apocalyptic sense of urgency and a timeless communion with the wisdom of God, gained through the insight the light gives us into the natural world. It would renew the traditional Quaker testimony of plain and simple living, within a horizon of concern for sustainable life on earth. Such a renewal, among Friends and elsewhere, must break out of the middle-class hall of mirrors that blinds us to our larger social and natural world. Something like "the kingdom of heaven," a realm of mutual amnesty and radical hospitality,[4] would be proclaimed and enacted. That kind of uprising was prefigured by the "Occupy" phenomenon that spontaneously sprouted and spread in cities around the world in 2011, combining religious and secular, middle-class and homeless people in protest and cooperative living. Meanwhile, in a rising sea of debt, ranging from personal finances to global finance, the term "forgiveness" may find new resonances in the years to come.

The localist movement is engendering a renewed sense of *place* and intimate relationship with the earth. Priority is given to food that is locally and organically grown. Local economic, social, and religious relationships find renewed symbiosis. The "transition" movement is bringing these elements together in some towns. These priorities unmask the bizarre unreality of global tourism, international trade, and electronic media diversions. Indeed, a vast variety of local and regional movements is spontaneously generating around the world to protect watersheds, rivers, bays, species, forests, indigenous peoples, and threatened cultural traditions against the onslaught of global capital and its reduction of everything in its path to market relations of equivalence and exchange.

In *Blessed Unrest* (2007), Paul Hawken suggests that these hundreds of thousands of nonviolent movements and initiatives may be understood as the earth, Gaia, working through us to defend, heal and renew herself, as her natural balances are pushed into crisis and dysfunction. Hawken compares these phenomena to the multiple immune systems of the body, working together in subtle ways to defend against the constant inroads of infection and toxicity. If we prefer, we can easily translate his thesis to suggest that the creative and re-creative wisdom of God is working through this amazing variety of groups to teach and restore human society to a sustainable relationship with the earth. The outcome of this global struggle is by no means assured. But when we become aware of the divine power available among us, we can avoid Sisyphean despair at the challenge we face. We live today in the balance of Wisdom's promise and warning: "And now my children, listen to me: happy are those who keep my ways. Hear instruction and be wise, and do not neglect it. Happy is the one who listens to me, watching daily at my gates, waiting beside my doors. For whoever finds me finds life and obtains favor from the Lord: but those who miss me injure themselves; all who hate me love death."

Friends have a significant role to play in this dispersed global phenomenon. Quaker faith and practice is outstanding in its ability to combine the prophetic and the wisdom streams of the Hebrew-Christian tradition. Eastern and animistic spiritualities are stronger in wisdom but weaker in the prophetic. Some western traditions are stronger in the prophetic but often cut off from wisdom, especially in the modern era. A renewed Quaker faith and practice can help the wider Christian church to reclaim its forgotten inheritance, to speak prophetically to the religious right that has captivated much of the Christian world. It can also bridge to other spiritual traditions that share our commitment to a sustainable life. Friends have a significant role to play in a convergence that still has no name.[5]

Wisdom from the Quaker Tradition

But we must first rediscover and reclaim that inheritance for ourselves. We heard in the Introduction to this book the many ways in which George Fox's spiritual transformation renewed his own relationship to the natural world and the divine wisdom that animates it. Fox then communicated this breakthrough to Seekers who felt bereft of relationship with God and with the earth. The plain, simple ways of Quaker speaking, dressing, and living emerged at the very beginning of the movement in 1652.

Charles Marshall was a teenaged Seeker in Bristol, England's second-largest city and a center of economic growth in 1654. He describes how his painful search for spiritual grounding and moral certainty drove him on long walks into the countryside. But even there:

> As I walked, and beheld the creation of God Almighty, every thing testified against me, heaven and earth, the day and the night, the sun, moon, and stars, yea, the watercourses and springs of the great deep, keeping in their respective places; and grass and flowers of the field, the fish of the sea and fowls of the air, keeping their order; but man fallen, the chief work of God's hand degenerated.[6]

Marshall describes wonder at the beauty and order of nature. But it only deepened his sense of being a stranger to its wisdom, of being "degenerated" from right relationship with God, with fellow humans, with the rest of creation.

Marshall was one of the many Bristol Seekers rocked by the Quaker preachers who arrived there in September 1654. Many were literally floored by the message and profoundly altered by the light's first work in them. One of them, Elizabeth Stirredge, likens the experience to the first day of creation: Thus began "the first day's work in my heart . . . to divide the light from the darkness [Gen. 1:3–5] and when the separation was made, then I could see my way in the light."[7] In other words, there was a way to go and a way to leave behind.

Stirredge recalls feeling threatened by the blunt, unadorned plainness of these northern Friends. But soon she and many others were compelled in the light to take similar steps. Marshall remembers,

> *Oh! the strippings of all needless Apparel, and the forsaking of superfluities in Meats, Drinks, and in the plain self-denying Path we walked . . . we were a plain broken-hearted, contrite-spirited, self-denying people . . . our Meetings were so large that we were forced to meet without doors . . . in Frost and Snow. . . . [The Lord] laid Judgment to the Line, and Righteousness to the Plummet [Isa. 28:17] . . . in mercy to our Poor Souls, that could not be redeemed but by Judgment poured out on the nature that had separated us from God.*[8]

Here again is the "plumb line" imagery that we noted in the preceding chapter. The peace of Quaker worship paradoxically induces an acute moral conflict. Early Quaker convincement was a difficult passage that drove Friends closer together in the solidarity of their struggle. Francis Howgill witnesses the experience of Westmoreland Seekers becoming Friends in 1652:

> *Our hearts were knit unto the Lord and one unto another in true and fervent love, in the covenant of Life with God; and that was a strong obligation or bond upon all our spirits, which united us one unto another. We met together in the unity of the Spirit, and of the bond of peace, treading down under our feet all reasoning about religion. . . . O happy day! O blessed day! the memorial of which can never pass out of my mind. And thus the Lord, in short, did form us to be a people for his praise in our generation.*[9]

Out of that deep struggle and joyful transformation, early Friends vigorously confronted the conformities of fashion in their day. In 1655, as he witnessed the lifestyles of the rich and famous in London, Fox published a paper that exclaimed:

What a world is this; how doth the devil garnish himself; how obedient are people to do his will and mind, that they are altogether carried with fooleries and vanities, both men and women, that they have lost the hidden man of the heart, the meek and quiet spirit, which is of the Lord, of great price. . . . Are not these the spoilers of creation and have the fat and best of it, and waste and destroy it?[10]

By contrast, Fox gently guided Friends and other tender spirits to the wisdom available in the light:

Wait all in the light for the wisdom by which all things were made, with it to use all the Lord's creatures to his glory . . . for which end they were created, and with the wisdom by which they were made, ye may be kept out of the misuse of them, in the image of God, that ye may come to see, that "the earth is the Lord's and the fullness thereof" [Ps. 24:1; 1 Cor. 10:26] *and the earth may come to yield her increase and enjoy her Sabbaths.*[11]

This creation-centered ethic included fair wages and conditions for employees, the humane use of animals, and moderate farming practices. The "master worker" who worked alongside God and was "daily delight" in the creation of the universe (recalling Proverbs 8) works with us today. Finding our right relation and sustainable life together on the earth is a matter of joy when we are grounded in the light and feel the power of God drawing us forward together.

Unfortunately, even vital breakthroughs may settle into hardened forms of custom. Over time, Quaker plainness and simplicity became a matter of rote, sectarian uniformity for many. By her late eighties, Margaret Fell had lived long enough to recognize and bemoan this tendency. She reminded Friends that in the Sermon on the Mount Jesus advised "that we must take no thought what we shall eat, or what we shall drink, or what we shall put on, but bids us consider the lilies how they grow. . . . But contrary to this . . . [today] we must be all in one dress and one color: this is a silly poor Gospel."[12]

Fortunately, through the centuries there have always been visionaries among Friends who restate the meaning of simplicity. John Woolman's words from *A Plea for the Poor* (1763), quoted in Chapter 5 in relation to equality and justice, are worth repeating here. They make the integral connections so clearly:

> *The Creator of the earth is the owner of it. He gave us being thereon, and our nature requires nourishment, which is the produce of it. As he is kind and merciful, we as his creatures, while we live answerable to the design of our creation, are so far entitled to a convenient subsistence that no man may justly deprive us of it. By the agreements and contracts of our fathers and predecessors, and by doings and proceedings of our own, some claim a much greater share of this world than others: and whilst those possessions are faithfully improved to the good of the whole, it consists with equity. But he who, with a view to self-exaltation, causeth some with their domestic animals to labour immoderately, and with monies arising to him therefrom, employs others in the luxuries of life, acts contrary to the gracious design of him who is the true owner of the earth; nor can any possessions, either acquired or derived from ancestors, justify such conduct.*[13]

Woolman is thus not categorically against the accumulation of wealth, but enjoins the privileged to apply their resources "to the good of the whole."

Thomas Clarkson, a leading English abolitionist and friend of Friends, wrote a three-volume *Portraiture of Quakerism* (1807) to interpret Quaker faith and practice to others. He notes in particular their

> *tender feelings toward brute creation. Animals are not considered mere machines, to be used at discretion, but in the sublime light as creatures of God, of whose existence the use*

and intention ought always to be considered, and to whom rights arise from various causes, and violation of which is a violation of moral law.[14]

The American Quaker minister Elias Hicks enjoyed hunting for sport in his early years, but gave it up as his growth in the light deepened his empathy and wisdom. He also came to question the systematic killing of wild animals in settled areas as "improvement of the wilderness." He reflects in his *Journal*, "We frequently err by the liberty we take in destroying what we esteem noxious creatures and not only abuse the power and rule given us over them by our great common Creator, but likewise act very contrary to and subversive of our own true interest."[15]

In a contemporary statement, North Carolina Yearly Meeting (Conservative) Friends witness the strong connection between integrity and simplicity:

> The heart of Quaker ethics is summed up in the word "simplicity." Simplicity is forgetfulness of self and remembrance of our humble status as waiting servants of God. Outwardly, simplicity is shunning superfluities of dress, speech, behavior and possessions, which tend to obscure our vision of reality. Inwardly, simplicity is spiritual detachment from the things of this world as part of the effort to fulfill the first commandment: to love God with all the heart and mind and strength.
>
> The testimony of outward simplicity began as a protest against the extravagance and snobbery which marked English society in the 1600s. In whatever forms this protest is maintained today, it must still be seen as a testimony against involvement with things which tend to dilute our energies and scatter our thoughts, reducing us to lives of triviality and mediocrity.
>
> Simplicity does not mean drabness or narrowness but is essentially positive, being the capacity for selectivity in one who holds attention on the goal. Thus simplicity is an appreciation of all that is helpful towards living as children of the Living God.[16]

When it arises from within, simplicity is not a burden but a liberation from the entanglements that clutter our homes, schedules, and consciousness. The *ethic* is also an *aesthetic*, a beauty that comes through clarity, economy of movement, and attention to detail.

Writing around 1940, Thomas Kelly framed "The Simplification of Life" mainly in terms of time management. He found Friends and others harried and distracted by too many concerns and commitments. This is still a problem today. But his comments apply just as well to the material distractions of consumer electronics, conspicuous consumption, waste, and pollution that press upon us and burden the creation today. Kelly stresses that simplicity must begin within:

We Western peoples are apt to think our great problems are external, environmental. We are not skilled in the inner life, where the real roots of our problem lie.... The outer distractions of our interests reflect an inner lack of integration in our own lives. We are trying to be several selves at once, without all our selves being organized into a single, mastering Life within us. Each of us tends to be, not a single self, but a whole committee of selves.

And we are unhappy, uneasy, strained, oppressed, and fearful we shall be shallow. For over the margins of life comes a whisper, a faint call, a premonition of richer living which we know we are passing by.... If only we could find the Silence which is the source of sound!

If the Society of Friends has anything to say, it lies in this region primarily. Life is meant to be lived from a Center, a divine Center. Each one of us can live such a life of amazing power and peace and serenity, of integration and confidence and simplified multiplicity, on one condition – that is, if we really want to.... We have not counted this Holy Thing within us to be the most precious thing in the world. We have not surrendered all else, to attend to it alone.

Many of the things we are doing seem so important to us. We haven't been able to say No to them, because they seemed so important. But if we center down, as the old phrase goes,

and live in that holy Silence which is dearer than life, and
take our life program into the silent places of the heart, with
complete openness, ready to do, ready to renounce according
to His leading, then many of the things we are doing lose their
vitality for us. I should like to testify to this, as a personal
experience, graciously given.[17]

Like North Carolina Friends, Kelly makes it clear that simplicity is a sustained life of *devotion*, training the human will to know and move with a divine will that must be "waited upon" day by day.[18]

Very few would wish to return to the uniform codes of traditional Quaker speech, dress, and lifestyle. Nevertheless, it seems clear, after a century and a half of Friends following (or evading) the testimonies on an individual basis, that we do need to query and lovingly challenge one another to take our devotion to a higher level. We do not need to adopt rote formulas. But could we work toward unity on "best practices" of simplicity and sustainable living among Friends?[19]

Jonathan Dale has been a prophetic voice among British Friends in recent decades. In *Quaker Social Testimony in Personal and Corporate Life* (2002), he laments that "testimony" has lost any serious meaning for Friends. It has been individualized and relativized to the extent that it offers no basis for corporate discernment of God's will. Friends have been "seduced by the dominant intellectual spirit of the age," reducing "Quakerism" to democracy, social progress, equality. Friends have lost the sense of a transcendent power in their lives. Dale reports his experience with a lifestyle sharing group in his monthly meeting near Manchester. They were careful to avoid becoming just another discussion group. They shared their experiences with changing personal habits. Some were more advanced and faithful than others. Members avoided judging one another or producing a single model for others to follow. Several made real changes in their lives. Much attention was paid to their practices of spending and giving away of money. One member of the group reflected,

On a personal level, the Life-style group was a way of getting
closer to people at meeting, and hearing about their personal
journeys. It made me more aware of the choices that I make
every day and what assumptions lie behind my actions (not

all of which are very Quakerly). I have made some changes in my life but I haven't, for example, got rid of my mobile phone. I haven't turned into an ascetic, nor do I think that this would be right for me. I've begun to realize, if only in a small way, the truth that the whole of our life is sacramental. Perhaps especially the boring, everyday bits (what we do with our rubbish, how we get to work, what we eat for our lunch).[20]

Dale also stresses the need for political action. For example, personal decisions about transportation need to be complemented by advocacy for better public transportation policies. Campaigning is a way of sharing our vision. Friends today leave this to our lobbying and social action organizations, but we need to add our own voices.

Meanwhile, in meeting life, coming into greater mutual accountability for our way of life rediscovers *covenant community*, the place where testimony is shared, refined, and enlarged *together*. Fear of accountability keeps our testimony locked in abstraction. But active group exploration works to overcome "liberal Quakerism's besetting sin of subjectivism."[21]

Dale reminds Friends of Fox's 1652 counsel (heard in Chapter 1 above) on following the demands of truth: "earthly reason shall tell you what you shall lose. Hearken not to that, but stand still in the Light, that shows them to you, and then strength comes from the Lord. And help, contrary to expectation." Dale concludes, "we need to use our testimonies as guides to another world than this one, here and now."[22]

British Friend Audrey Urry (1994) describes that other world Dale urges us toward:

All species and the Earth itself have interdependent roles within Creation. Humankind is not the species, to whom all others are subservient, but one among many. All parts, all issues, are inextricably intertwined. Indeed the web of creation could be described as of three-ply thread: wherever we touch it we affect justice and peace and the health of all everywhere. So all our testimonies, all our Quaker work, all our Quaker lives are part of one process, of striving toward a flourishing, just and peaceful Creation.[23]

Urry is of course right that we are "but one among many" species. And yet we have clearly become the dominant species of the earth, with tremendous powers for good and evil in creation. In Genesis 1:28 God blesses human "dominion" of the creation "in our image" (God's and creation's). To have *dominion* is to act in the wisdom of a higher authority *in* the creation. To *dominate* is to exert sheer personal power *over* the creation. To grow into our true dominion among the creatures, we must move from acting as dominators to serving as *stewards* of the earth, tending its life-sustaining balances and conserving its resources.

Hence, *stewardship* constitutes the middle term between a personal ethic of *simplicity* and a present-day concern for the *sustainability* of life on this planet. The steward (in Greek, *oikonomikos*, the root of our words "economy" and "ecology") manages the finances and resources of the house with an economical sense of the whole. As good stewards we develop an economy of time, energy, and resource use, with an eye to the life of the whole planet. Life in community with others fosters more economical living and builds peaceful, symbiotic relationships with neighboring individuals, communities, and organizations.

Quaker Faith and Practice: Timely and Timeless

Urry's image of the three-ply thread suggests that we might represent the dynamics of stewardship as a third axis added to the two axes we contemplated in the preceding chapter (see chart on facing page).

In this three-dimensional perspective, equality/community remains the vertical "plumb line" of personal morality and social justice revealed among us when we enter the peace of "standing still in the light." As noted in the preceding chapter, that acute moral and social sense, strengthened by our experience of egalitarian community, compels us to *prophetic* nonviolent witness for justice and equality. But the light also reveals the *wisdom* of God and reconnects us with the creation. So the same moral plumb line compels us to move toward a more sustainable relationship with the earth and to advocate politically for the earth and its species.

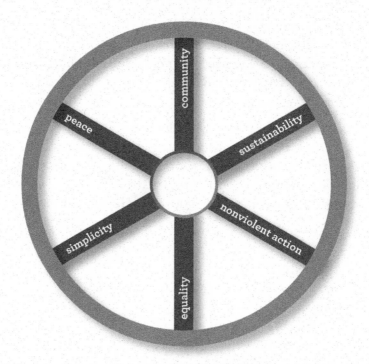

A fourth dimension is implied by the dynamic interaction of the other three: that of *time/movement*. All of these factors are in motion, in constant interaction. Each element continuously reinforces but also questions, qualifies, and redefines the others. So, at the still center of the triple axes there is the timelessness of eternity we experience in waiting upon the Lord, individually or together. Still, that stillness is brimming with dynamism. The divine life activates us to faithful lives as witnesses for God's peace and justice, as wise stewards God's creation. Day by day our faith and practice draw us "in time, up to God, out of time, through time."

Advices and Queries from Britain Yearly Meeting's *Quaker Faith & Practice*

#39: Consider which of the ways to happiness offered by society are truly fulfilling and which are potentially corrupting and destructive. Be discriminating when choosing means of entertainment and information. Resist the desire to acquire possessions or income through unethical investment, speculation or games of chance.

#41: Try to live simply. A simple lifestyle freely chosen is a source of strength. Do not be persuaded into buying what you do not need or cannot afford. Do you keep yourself informed about the effects your style of living is having on the global economy and environment?

#42: We do not own the world, and its riches are not ours to dispose of at will. Show a loving consideration for all creatures, and seek to maintain the beauty and variety of the world. Work to ensure that our increasing power over nature is used responsibly, with reverence for life. Rejoice in the splendor of God's continuing creation.

CONCLUSION

The Sustainable Friends Meeting: Occupy!

The chapters of this book have explored Quaker faith and practice as the dynamic interaction of sixteen energies along eight axes. These may be represented as the radii or spokes of a turning wheel (see chart on facing page).

Each of the sixteen factors in faith and practice needs its counterpart to remain a healthy spiritual energy. And each of the eight axes is informed by the other seven, to produce a dynamic matrix of life. The whole is a conjoining of spiritual and material forces that are our inheritance, as we live into our potential as the image of both God and the universe. The empty center represents the place of unknowing we experience as we live within these tensions and paradoxes. Here dwells the divine presence, the "I am that I am," who abides beyond all our definitions, but who calls us into the life of communion-and-community, a stillness-and-action that embodies all these paradoxes. We never abide perfectly at the center. Our personal conditions and our lived circumstances buffet us. But as we remain patient with ourselves and with one another in faith and practice, the center keeps drawing us "in time, up to God, out of time, through time." In other words, as we sustain faith with one another and with the practices we hold together in trust, we find ourselves sustained by a power that is beyond the sum of all these parts.

But what might this sustainable faith and practice look like in the life of a Friends meeting today? In many cases, it may not be very different from the faith and practice Friends already sustain. But let us now review the eight axes identified in the chapters of this book, to describe the sustainable Friends meeting, and suggest ways that meetings may become more sustainable.

Along the way, we will supplement sustain with the more overtly active verb occupy. A faith and practice equal to the enormous challenges of the twenty-first century will be more energized than "sustainability" might suggest. I am of course informed by the recent Occupy movement, which burst forth in cities and towns around the world in 2011, in response to the financial debacle that began in 2008. Occupy asserted the rights and needs of the 99% against the buccaneering financial designs of the richest 1%, the capitalist institutions that serve them, and the governmental policies that facilitate their continual raids upon the common treasury of natural resources, human labor, and tax dollars. The spontaneous occupation of parks and squares near Wall Street, other financial centers, and government buildings gave the movement its name.

But like "sustainability," the verb "occupy" has larger resonances that we will explore here. The modern English word comes from the Latin *cupare*, which means "to take hold." "To occupy" has three principal definitions: to engage the mind, to fill a space, or to seize a territory. The following exploration of faith and practice today embraces all three meanings.

Light and Seed: *Quaker Spiritual Practice*

Chapter 1 explored the deeper registers of Quaker spiritual formation, the daily personal practices that ground us in the divine presence, that allow us to come to meeting for worship "with hearts and minds prepared" to contribute to the collective practice of Quaker worship and ministry. Spiritual formation is what Brother Lawrence called "the practice of the presence of God." It is the work of becoming more consistently awake to the Spirit in the here and now of our lives (present to the presence in the present moment). We explored that practice in terms of the two principal guiding images of traditional Quaker counsel: light and seed. Light suggests revealing and knowing, while seed suggests being and willing. These two aspects of the divine presence interact and strengthen one another, so that we grow in understanding, in compassion, and in an active, faithful life. Through our Quaker spiritual practice we befriend God within. We allow divine love and wisdom to *occupy* our hearts and minds. And in so doing, we *occupy* our bodies in new ways. In standing still in the light, sinking down to the seed, we learn to register God's presence and guidance. The whole body, not just the heart or mind, becomes the registering instrument. We learn a physical stillness that engenders mental quiet and emotional peace. Until then, we are *pre*-occupied by endless thoughts and feelings, both pleasant and unpleasant. And in this new century, the endless seductions of electronic devices have taken preoccupation to a whole new level.

Unfortunately, the spiritual guidance to help us occupy our bodies and sustain fruitful life is all too rare in most Friends meetings today. We welcome all to share in our worship and activities. We try to make everyone as comfortable as possible, hoping that they will find their spiritual home with us. But the unquiet silence in many meetings for worship, rambling and unedifying vocal ministry, and digressive business meetings suggest that even many longtime members and attenders have not learned the disciplines of daily spiritual practice. Some newcomers stay for a while and then drift away. Others stay, but find helpful guidance from other traditions: Buddhist meditation, yoga, Christian monastic practices, and so on. And others simply adopt the same casual bad habits they have learned from the apparent "leading lights" of the meeting.

But Friends have a powerful spiritual practice, as demonstrated by the writers quoted in Chapter 1. It is less a matter of steps in a technique than locating and occupying a certain inward space where one learns to find refreshment, guidance, and communion with the divine. Some meetings have used Rex Ambler's Experiment with Light as a regular group exercise outside meeting for worship, to help with individual discernment and to deepen the spiritual life of the meeting.

The sustainable Friends meeting will help its participants find the spiritual *sustenance* they need, not only to sustain their roles in the meeting, but also to empower their personal lives of work, witness, and service in the world. Newcomers and longstanding Friends can explore together resources in Quaker literature such as Rex Ambler's anthology of Fox's spiritual counsel, *Truth of the*

Heart, modern Quaker classics such as Thomas Kelly's *Testament of Devotion*, Sandra Cronk's *Dark Night Journey*, or Brian Drayton's *Getting Rooted*, and contemporary guides such as Patricia Loring's *Listening Spirituality* (vol. 1). But the spiritual practices of other traditions may also prove valuable, not only for personal sustainability but also to build spiritual bridges with the wider human family.

Ministers and elders in the local meeting (formally recognized as such or not) need to offer guidance and encouragement, not just affirmation and acceptance. Like the seed that fell on stony ground in Jesus's parable of the sower (Mark 4:19), if the root does not find its way to depth, the tender plant will be choked by competing concerns. Of course, to offer that kind of help, ministers and elders need to sustain a regular spiritual practice of their own. That practice requires patience with oneself, which in turn strengthens the compassionate receptivity toward others that discerns the real need behind the stated concern and finds the words that speak most helpfully to that need. Just as casual dress has come to substitute for plain dress among modern Friends, so casual friendliness has come to substitute for the plain-spoken directness that truly ministers to one another's needs, even if it isn't always comfortable to speak or to hear. A life that is spiritually sustainable for us as individuals, collectively sustainable for our meetings, and that leads to sustainable patterns of life on earth, must see through the myriad delusions and cut through the entangling habituations of a consumer-driven culture. Are we living sustainably?

Worship and Ministry: *A Prophetic People*

There are calls rising among Friends today for "prophetic ministry," though one seldom hears what is meant by the term, other than depth of conviction and courage of expression. Those are important hallmarks, but Chapter 2 of this book drew from both the richness of Quaker tradition and the biblical prophets themselves to suggest that Friends are indeed called to be a prophetic people. Prophetic ministry grows out of the depth of spiritual practice described above. The Hebrew prophet Jeremiah (Jer. 23:18, 22) knew how to "stand in the council of the Lord" to receive a word to speak to his people. The prophet Isaiah (Isa, 40:31) learned how to "wait upon the Lord" and receive strength and conviction, while others fainted with exhaustion and despair. George Fox counseled bewildered seekers to "stand still in the light" and receive wisdom and strength "contrary to your expectation."

William Taber emphasized that prophetic ministry consists as much in our expectant silence and compassionate listening as in our speaking in worship. Indeed, our most experienced "weighty" Friends model prophetic ministry as much by the quality of their stillness as by the quantity of their messages in meeting. The purpose of Quaker worship was never that "everyone can have a say." Instead, *no one* should speak, except to be "spoken through" by a Word and wisdom from beyond themselves. This advice can inhibit vocal ministry in unhelpful ways. But a too-easy affirmation of whatever is said in meeting often moves Quaker worship into the realm of worship sharing. While the latter practice is quite useful for an informal airing of our different views and concerns, the former is a high calling. There is a spiritual *authority* that occupies the gathered group, and a sense of awe is appropriate. Again, casualness and trying to make everyone comfortable are not helpful. Outside the meeting house is a world of violence, exploitation, and degradation. We gather to offer sanctuary to one another in the sanctuary of God's presence, which is our only hope of living courageously and sustainably out there.

The matrix of characteristics of prophetic ministry charted in Chapter 2 may be useful in locating the spiritual *place* where ministry may arise in a given moment. But more importantly, worship and ministry in the manner of Friends, repeated again and again over time, establish the shared place in space and time that sustains all our faith and practice. The Quaker use of the term "meeting" implies both the group that gathers and the event of their gathering. The "meeting house" is the physical place we maintain within the grid of space-time that our capitalist society continuously transforms in its relentless processes of "creative destruction" (that is, the changing array of houses, shopping centers, office buildings, and so on that surround the meeting house). The sustainable Friends meeting begins ever anew in occupying that place, imbuing it with spiritual depth and ethical boundaries, within a grid where market values determine almost everything.

In his book, *The Land*, Old Testament scholar Walter Brueggemann defines "place" as

> *space which has historical meanings, where some things have happened which are now remembered, which provide continuity and identity across generations. Place is a space in which important words have been spoken which established identity, defined vocation, and envisioned destiny. Place is space in which vows have been exchanged, promises have been made, and demands have been issued. Place is indeed a protest against the unpromising pursuit of space. It is a declaration that your humanness cannot be found in escape, detachment, absence of commitment, and undefined freedom.[1]*

The sustained practice of place is where we come "back to earth" in faithful, covenantal relationship with the other humans and with other species in and around that place. Our shared practice of the "covenant of light," begins to reweave the web of a sustainable life. Conversely, an ungrounded concern for "sustainability" will be fretful and misplaced.

Hence, the sustainable Friends meeting will maintain and remodel its meeting house in resource-efficient patterns. These not only merge spiritual and material practices into a single, sustained life, but also serve as a model, a teaching site for others in the neighborhood and wider community. The meeting house is integral to the meeting for worship. So the sustainable Friends meeting integrates the work of ministers and elders, trustees and finance committees, with the support and encouragement of all active members, to establish a fully occupied place of spirit and truth. It is the place where, as William Penn advised, we are changed as persons before we go out to change the world.

Personal Integrity and Discernment: *"Mind the Oneness"*

Sustained personal spiritual practice and meetings for worship gradually work to integrate us as persons. We more fully *occupy* the unique personality we were created to be. This is fully realized only in community with others. Words we once spoke carelessly and actions we took in emulation of others begin to fall away. They are needless and bothersome clutter, self-defeating habits that have impeded our progress in being who we are and following our calling in life. This integration into unified personhood is itself a testimony to the transcendent One who created us and who calls us to a beautiful destiny.

Today more than ever, integrity is a courageous stand against the proliferating gadgetry and diversions of an intensely mediated culture (television, film, the internet, and so on). We start out thinking we are fashioning a unique self out of all these consumer options and instant information, when in fact we are being led around by the nose into mindless conformity. As Chel Avery observes, "it is a conformity to ways our attention is engaged, by a constant barrage of cute messages, shocking messages, heart wrenching messages, one after another. So while we are constantly making personal choices (I like this – don't like that; want this – don't want that), the choices are fished out of a pool that is very wide but very shallow, as is the quality of our attention."[2] To "mind the oneness," using the old Quaker phrase, is first to find that One and then to follow it into what Parker Palmer has called "the undivided life."

The examples from John Woolman's *Journal* in Chapter 3 remind us that often the journey into greater integrity begins with a painful experience of acting without integrity, knuckling under to the expectations of others, seeking acceptance from peers. But like Woolman, we can redeem these failures, bend that pain of conscience to the service of new, creative patterns of faithfulness. Again like Woolman, we will need at times to draw upon the wisdom of others in our meeting to help us make important decisions, through the use of clearness committees and informal conversations. The matrix of considerations charted in Chapter 3 for use in personal discernment, with or without a clearness committee, may be helpful in keeping the wider range of considerations in view, so that our life decisions enact our commitment to a sustainable world.

And as we nurture one another toward greater personal integrity, we can expect that our solidarity with one another will only grow. Thomas Gates emphasizes that the Friends meeting should actively nurture the *expectation* that one will receive divine leadings, and actively support its members in clarifying and following them. Formal membership only *begins* a lifelong process whereby individuals grow and change in relation to the meeting community — or else stagnate or drift away. "In Quaker faith and practice, the individual and the meeting are in a dynamic, mutually supportive, and reciprocal relation." True individuality arises "within the matrix of a supportive and nurturing community."[3] Again, integrity-in-community occupies a distinctive *place* in the wider social grid. The sustainable Friends meeting can reach out in dialogue and cooperative action with other communities of integrity. But integrity is as idiomatic to communities as it is to individuals, and we must continually work at strengthening the shared integrity that is unique to *this* meeting in *this* place.

These different dynamic aspects of Quaker faith and practice are all foundational to one another. They all become easier as we do any one of them better. Conversely, our neglect of any one of them can harbor weaknesses and unexamined motives that wreak havoc with all the others. Mistakes will happen. We will not act with integrity in every case. *Forgiveness* is a powerful force in reweaving tears in the fabric of the sustainable Friends meeting. Talking through our conflicts, admitting to our mistakes, and forgiving others for theirs not only allows us to go on. We are actually made stronger through these trespasses. The sustainable Friends meeting is the place where we forgive but do not forget. The memories may make us wince or weep, but sometimes they also make us laugh together.

Equality and Community: *Testimony in Conversation*

Chapter 4 explored the deep interrelation between equality and community, two "testimonies" we usually consider separately. The place of the Friends meeting is located on a social grid that tends to divide people according to racial and ethnic identities, class interests, religious and cultural sensibilities, and so on. Across those divisions, people often view one another with suspicion and fear, based mostly in ignorance. And those forms of social alienation promote and perpetuate many forms of inequality, injustice, economic exploitation, and violence.

But the Friends meeting is a community where we learn to "regard no one from a human point of view" (2 Cor. 5:16). We reach to "that of God in every one" from the knowledge of God within ourselves. The sustainable meeting is a place where we create sanctuary for one another against the corrosive spirits of racism, classism, and prejudice around us. Like Isaiah, we find that sanctuary first of all in God:

> *For the Lord spoke thus to me while his hand was strong upon me, and warned me not to walk in the way of this people, saying: Do not call conspiracy all that this people calls conspiracy, and do not fear what it fears, nor be in dread. But the Lord of hosts, him you shall regard as holy, let him be your fear, and let him be your dread. He will become a sanctuary, a stone one strikes against* [Isa. 8:11-14].

"Fear" and "dread" of God are better translated as "awe." It is a practiced sense of God's sustaining love, which gradually displaces our fear of one another.[4] It is a peace the world cannot give (John 14:27), nor understand. Hence, the sanctuary we experience together and extend to others is at times scandalous, a stumbling stone to those who do not know it. Indeed, the indiscriminate practice of friendship is subversive. For 350 years Friends have scandalized others, from the partnership of male and female leaders at the beginning of our movement, to the inclusion of persons of different races, sexual orientations, and transgendered identities today. Certainly, we have not practiced friendship perfectly or consistently. But as love keeps casting out fear, we grow bolder in whom and how we love. Again, the more awe we feel in God's presence, the less fear we feel toward others.

The late Jim Corbett's work with the sanctuary movement in the American Southwest during the 1980s exemplifies the interaction of equality and community.[5] A Quaker rancher in southern Arizona, he began encountering political refugees from Central America out in the desert where he herded goats. In befriending and seeking to help them, he was drawn into ecumenical cooperation with a variety of churches and other groups, creating a sanctuary network to house and protect refugees, in violation of federal law. Their practice of what Corbett called *civil initiative* asserted the human rights of those the state refused to recognize. Such activities, legal and illegal, rebuild society from the base. Political advocacy and legal action are important to extending sanctuary of any kind. But most of all, civil initiative is the constant interaction of equality and community. The work for equality creates new forms of community, while community folds new social identities into its matrix of equitable interaction.

The conversation between Jesus and the Samaritan woman in John 4 is instructive. Their dialogue unfolds across differences in gender, ethnicity, and religious affiliation. They converge at a "place" that is neither his people's nor her people's holy shrine, but "spirit and truth." Quaker worship is an attempt to meet at that place, beyond creeds and liturgical forms. But we must be ever vigilant that our Quaker faith and practice does not slip into the Eurocentrism of its English beginnings or the cultural preferences, university-educated intellectualism, and middle-class mannerisms of the European American majority of Friends in North America. If we are not mindful of these encroaching norms, we will marginalize and repel those who do not fit comfortably. Yes, we come from different places on the social grid. But when we truly meet at a place of "spirit and truth," "there is no longer Jew or Greek, there is no longer slave or free, there is no longer male and female" (Gal. 3:28).

The sustainable Friends meeting offers sanctuary to all kinds of people, in confidence that our faith and practice will be a homecoming for some. Others may find their home in other communities and spiritual traditions. But we do no one a service by undervaluing the unique spiritual genius of our tradition. If maintaining numbers or growth is a concern, it is good for Friends to remember that the movements that gain most adherents today, from Buddhism to Mormons, are those that challenge people to stretch. Have we become too comfortable?

Ministers, Elders, Clerks, and Group Discernment: *The Peaceable Kingdom*

The fabric of the sustainable Friends meeting is woven from the warp and weft of equality and community. The Quaker endeavor to make decisions together in unity is the greatest expression of that process, which integrates the insights and leadings of each of us into a whole greater than the sum of the parts. Indeed, "Quaker process" is not simply how we conduct our decision making as groups. It is the way *all* of Quaker faith and practice undergirds our work in finding unity. The meeting (for worship with a concern) for business is redolent with backstory. In a healthy, sustainable meeting, it is the "sweet savor" of many faithful searches together, where conflicts were overcome, where new insights were welcomed, where hurts were acknowledged and forgiven. In an unhealthy meeting, it is the miasma of unresolved grudges, unredeemed egos, and petty attitudes. This enervated condition results in superficial worship, lowest common denominator decision making, and lack of outreach or social witness.

During the first half of our history, Quaker worship and business became overly dominated by the official ministers and elders of the meeting. By the mid-nineteenth century, evangelical and liberal renewals began to open vocal ministry and business process to greater participation. As early as 1865, a British Friend noted happily that attendance at yearly meeting had tripled. But with mixed feelings, he noted that sessions "consist no longer of Friends sitting in awe of the meeting and rising with fear and trembling to speak, but of men accustomed to vivacious discussions."[6] The freedom of that new phase was no doubt exhilarating. But while "vivacious discussions" may stimulate the mind and cheer the heart, they tend to scamper off in many directions. They do not arise from that deeper place that regular spiritual practice trains us to occupy. And over time, they run roughshod over sensitive individuals, trenchant concerns, and deeper insights. People get hurt, truth gets lost among opinions and personal preferences, and often no one takes time to pick up the pieces.

The pendulum has swung far from the dominating leadership of two centuries ago. Distrust of leadership has become reflexive, sometimes petulant. "Unity" has been sentimentalized into more a feeling than a hard-won sense of shared meaning, purpose, and direction. Few are courageous enough to exercise leadership except in the most oblique and unrecognized ways. The liberation from the repressive leadership of the early nineteenth century has become a new form of captivity. The current state of the Society is unsustainable. It cannot empower Friends to be agents for a sustainable future on earth.

The ability of meetings to make difficult and costly decisions together rarely generates spontaneously. It must be nurtured by those more experienced in seeking truth in the manner of Friends, individuals who recognize and gently expose the delusions of the mind and secret motives of the heart. The meeting also requires men and women who can articulate and advance the shared vision of the meeting, who can connect it with the deeper Christian roots of Quaker faith and the biblical saga that gave rise to it. Whether it formally recognizes "elders" and "ministers" or not, the meeting resists the witness and nurture of such Friends at its own risk. Leaving it to clerks to wrest unity out of confusion will rarely succeed.

The sustainable Friends meeting will encourage gifted members in developing their gifts through study and training, both formal and informal, to grow into the roles of ministers, elders, and clerks. We have great, but underutilized resources. Pendle Hill, the Earlham School of Religion, Woodbrooke, and the School of the Spirit offer both short- and longer-term training in spiritual nurture, clerkship, and various forms of ministry. Of course, those growing into such roles must retain a servant-sense of their work under the care of the meeting.[7]

Unity and Differentiation:
Learning from Quaker Diversity

Chapter 6 offered an overview of Quaker history, which needs no further comment here. But the history offers background to the surprising diversity of Friends today. When we recognize different branches of Friends as the fruit of different renewals in Quaker history, we are less likely to view other kinds of Quaker faith and practice as random acts of violence against "my Quakerism." Certainly, most Friends strongly prefer their own meeting's version of faith and practice and would find it difficult to participate with some other varieties. But there are some — indeed, a growing number — who find themselves positively drawn to the variety of Friends.

My own background is in pastoral Quakerism in the Midwest, and I have served as a Friends pastor off and on over the years. But I also find myself at home in the unprogrammed streams of Friends.[8] I have also learned much from four years among British Friends, and from work with Kenyan and Latin American Friends at Pendle Hill and the Earlham School of Religion. There are riches everywhere among Friends, if we have eyes open to see them and hearts open to embrace them.

As suggested in Chapter 6, our evangelical and liberal streams of faith and practice represent major desertions from traditional Quakerism as well as significant renewals of it. Conservative Friends, too, have evolved, even as they have sought more carefully than the rest of us to retain traditional faith and practice. This phenomenon is part of being a living species of spiritual life, adapting to changing social terrains and cultural climates. The sustainable Friends meeting will find itself on a larger map of the Quaker extended family, and learn to embrace differences, even if we never fully understand some of those distant cousins. The Friends World Committee for Consultation continues to invite the world family of Friends into mutual encounter and dialogue. Various more recent initiatives have also been fruitful. Convergent Friends have promoted dialogue mainly via the internet. Quaker Voluntary Service brings a variety of younger Friends together in social service projects and communal living. And young adult Friends gatherings challenge the prejudices that older generations of Friends have too seldom questioned. A sustainable world family of Friends will be mindful of the carbon footprint that wide-ranging travel leaves. But we will continue finding new ways to interconnect.

Peace and Nonviolent Action: *The Lamb's War*

Chapter 7 suggested that the peace we find through regular spiritual practice and meeting for worship reveals a "plumb line," a heightened sense of personal morality and social justice. In turn, that vertical axis reveals a perpendicular axis, in which the peace of inward communion is balanced by a call to nonviolent action, to confront the personal and social wrongs revealed by the plumb line. The larger prophetic vocation of Friends generates from this spiritual compass. We feel compelled to change things in our own lives, and to speak and act for justice. Our witness may be conciliatory or confrontational. It may fall within legal boundaries of political conduct, or it may cross over into witness that peacefully breaks the law. Jim Corbett's preference of the term "civil initiative" over "civil disobedience" is helpful. Our goal is to *initiate* a more just, peaceful, and sustainable society. Obedience or disobedience is a secondary matter. But nonviolence of words and actions is essential. Our means and ends must be harmonious. A sustainable world must be advanced in ways that sustain life.

The sustainable Friends meeting speaks with confidence and patience to the authorities and powers around it, because it is grounded in the peace of its own faith and practice. That peace sustains social witness in ways that more agitated and alienated mind states cannot. It subversively befriends opponents that others might consider enemies. The meeting's peace and social concerns committee plays an important leadership role. But it should not view itself as the bearer of the meeting's social conscience. Rather, its work is to nurture concerns as they arise from the meeting, helping to build wider support in the meeting for action. Rather than a group sequestered with a particular job description on behalf of the meeting, the committee (indeed, any meeting committee) serves best by drawing others together around a few concerns that can be sustained over time. Otherwise, the meeting will be overwhelmed and paralyzed by a litany of worldly woes.

Particular attention should be paid to concerns of justice, equality, and violence on the local level. This is important for grounding the meeting's sense of place in its social community and natural habitat. It builds stronger relations with the neighborhood, local government, and the underserved. This is not to ignore the problems of the wider world. But a highly mediated culture like our own *preoccupies* us with many problems too distant for us to respond to usefully. The task of the sustainable meeting is to *occupy* its place more resolutely, to give its service to truth greater social texture through local cooperation and neighborliness.

Finally, through lifestyle discussion groups and meeting threshing sessions, the sustainable meeting uses the queries gently to help members live into greater congruence between their concerns and their actual way of life. Over the past century, Friends have sometimes become as doctrinaire in their social and political views as many were in the nineteenth century over religious tenets (see Chapter 6). A deeper search is required to become "the same in life as in words." The advice to examine "whatever in your own way of life may contain the seeds of war" is a lifelong, 360-degree challenge for all of us. We need one another's help, encouragement, and example. Can we find productive ways to answer the queries again?

Simplicity and Sustainability: *Daily Delight*

To review briefly, we occupy our bodies more fully as we become more wholly present in the moment. This regular spiritual practice attunes the body as the registering instrument for the light's teaching and leading. As we bring that attunement to the meeting for worship, the group begins to occupy the place of spirit and truth more consistently and resolutely. Words spoken out of the silence come from that place and define that place more explicitly in the group. Over time, the experience draws participants into a clearer sense of their identity and purpose, shedding unnecessary, unhealthy, or immoral habits, integrating the personality. The sustainable meeting helps individuals in that process of personal discernment through clearness committees, personal mentoring, and in other ways. Important decisions serve as moments of truth, in which a new sense of purpose may make the renunciation of useless attachments easier. As that sense of place becomes stronger in the meeting community, it draws people from different places on the social grid into encounter with one another. We both affirm and transcend our differences as we "know one another in that which is eternal."

Meanwhile, the meeting gradually functions better in sensing and following God's will together, because its members are becoming more themselves and more willingly transparent to one another. But this does not happen automatically. Catalysts in the roles of ministers, elders, and clerks (whether recognized as such or not) help individuals and groups work through delusions, resistances, and grudges. The more healthy and nondefensive the meeting becomes, the more it is able to see beyond itself and appreciate its place in the wider family of Friends. It also values the ways the Quaker family has been influenced by the wider family of the church, by other religions, and by secular society. It is true that in many cases, wider influences have eroded the unique place of Quaker faith and practice. But they have also enabled collaborative connections across religious boundaries in the work for justice and peace. And those connections have allowed the prophetic witness of Friends to influence a variety of religious and social change groups. Early Friends were great innovators in nonviolent action for peace and justice in the early modern period. We continue to exercise that genius in pioneering ways.

Friends have also embodied a deep synthesis of prophetic social vision and earth-based wisdom. Friends have traditionally been more connected with God's wisdom in nature than most Christian traditions, and more prophetic in social witness than most non-Christian traditions. The Introduction and Chapter 8 of this book have attempted to reacquaint Friends with just how profoundly our spiritual formation, grounded in the body, connects us with the earth. And the book overall weaves that forgotten strength into the larger synthesis of our faith and practice.[9]

As the sustainable Friends meeting occupies the place of spirit and truth with growing clarity and purpose, the interaction between personal simplification and work for a sustainable world will help the meeting "think globally and act locally." We are still learning how appreciate and enact that familiar adage. In this century, a *localist* ethic of food production and consumption, organizational collaboration, and responses to poverty, violence, and resource depletion will prove foundational to all other earth care and social witness. The alienating effects of global capitalism — which hides the unjust and violent relations of production, encourages waste of energy and other resources, and makes us strangers to our own neighbors — can be resisted only through renewed local focus.

As we occupy our localities more intentionally, we begin to withdraw our cooperation with the global regime of hypercapitalist forces that drive it. The banking and corporate power centers that dominate and degrade the natural and social landscape will slowly be isolated and disempowered. Along the way, the gated communities that protect the 1% from the rest of us will protect the rest of us from the 1%. These processes will probably be accelerated and intensified by further economic reversals, which accompany the parasitical practices of the banking industry and the government policies that facilitate them. These developments may prove disastrous for many. And Friends will need to be responsive in meeting desperate human needs. It is the end of a world, whose form is already passing away.

As we saw in George Fox's 1648 experience (see Introduction), a flaming sword stands at the gate to the garden. Re-entry is a harrowing passage. If Friends are willing to pass through that flame together, we have an important role to play in the renewal of creation and in the social revolution that clears the space for it. Not only were early Friends the first great innovators of nonviolent direct action for social change in the modern era. They were also the first to create a spiritual basis for a modern multicultural and interfaith society. They also innovated a unique covenantal organizational structure that places central authority and local autonomy in creative (if not always easy) interaction. These are important precedents for a grassroots social revolution that can meet the challenges of this century. The problem is, *we have forgotten the revolutionary thrust of these Quaker hallmarks.* Settling into sectarian perpetuation, the social norms around us have slowly seeped in and neutralized Quaker faith and practice, to make it a rather comfortable religion.

What does a revolutionary Quaker faith and practice sound like? Try this sound-bite from George Fox in July 1663, as persecutions reached a fever pitch and Friends by the thousands suffered fines, imprisonments, and violence. During a break between his own imprisonments, Fox wrote these lines to the movement:

> *Sing and rejoice, ye children of the day and of the light; for the Lord is at work in this thick night of darkness that may be felt. And truth doth flourish as the rose, and the lilies do grow among the thorns, and the plants atop the hills, and upon them the lambs do skip and play. And never heed the tempests nor the storms, floods nor rains, for the seed Christ is over all, and doth reign. And so be of good faith and valiant for the truth: for the truth can live in the jails. And fear not the loss of the fleece, for it will grow again; and follow the lamb, if it be under the beast's horns, or under the beast's heels; for the lamb shall have the victory over them all.*[10]

WORKS CITED

Adams, Anne. *Is There Not a New Creation? The Experience of Early Friends*. Leominster, Herefordshire: Orphans Press, 2012.

Ambler, Rex. *Truth of the Heart: An Anthology of George Fox*. London: Quaker Books, 2001.

———. *Light To Live By: An Exploration in Quaker Spirituality*. London: Quaker Books, 2002.

Barbour, Hugh and J. William Frost. *The Quakers*. New York: Greenwood Press, 1988.

Barbour, Hugh and Arthur O. Roberts. *Early Quaker Writings, 1650-1700*. Wallingford, PA: Pendle Hill Publications, 2004.

Benson, Lewis. "On Being Moved by the Spirit to Minister in Public Worship" in *The Quaker Vision*. Gloucester: New Foundation, 1979.

Birkel, Michael. *A Near Sympathy: The Timeless Quaker Wisdom of John Woolman*. Richmond, IN: Friends United Press, 2003.

Bownas, Samuel. *A Description of the Qualifications Necessary to a Gospel Minister* (1750). Wallingford, PA: Pendle Hill Publications, 1989.

Braithwaite, William, C. *The Beginnings of Quakerism*, 2nd ed. Cambridge: Cambridge University Press, 1970.

Brinton, Howard. *Reaching Decisions: The Quaker Method*, Pendle Hill Pamphlet #65. Wallingford, PA: Pendle Hill Publications, 1952.

Brock, Peter. *The Quaker Peace Testimony, 1660-1914*. York: Sessions, 1990.

Britain Yearly Meeting of Friends. *Quaker Faith & Practice: The Christian Book of Discipline*. London: Quaker Books, 1995.

Brueggemann, Walter. *The Land: Place as Gift, Promise, and Challenge in Biblical Faith*. Philadelphia: Fortress Press, 1977.

Buckley, Paul. *The Essential Elias Hicks*. San Francisco: Inner Light Books, 2013.

Cooper, Wilmer. *The Testimony of Integrity*, Pendle Hill Pamphlet #296. Wallingford, PA: Pendle Hill Publications, 1991.

Corbett, Jim. *Goatwalking: A Guide to Wildland Living, a Quest for the Peaceable Kingdom.* New York: Viking Press, 1991.

—————. *The Sanctuary Church*, Pendle Hill Pamphlet #270. Wallingford, PA: Pendle Hill Publications, 1987.

Cornell, Andrew. *Oppose and Propose! Lessons from Movement for a New Society.* Oakland, CA: AK Press, 2011.

Craig, Clarence Tucker. "Commentary on 1 Corinthians" in George Arthur Buttrick, ed., *The Interpreter's Bible*, vol. 10. Nashville, TN: Abingdon Press, 1953.

Cronk, Sandra. *Dark Night Journey: Inward Repatterning Toward a Life Centered in God.* Wallingford, PA: Pendle Hill Publications, 1991.

—————. *Gospel Order: A Quaker Understanding of Faithful Church Community*, Pendle Hill Pamphlet #297. Wallingford, PA: Pendle Hill Publications, 1991.

Dale, Jonathan. *Quaker Social Testimony in Personal and Corporate Life*, Pendle Hill Pamphlet #360. Wallingford, PA: Pendle Hill Publications, 2002.

Dandelion, Pink. *A Sociological Analysis of the Theology of Quakers: The Silent Revolution.* Lampeter, Wales: Mellen, 1996.

Doncaster, L. Hugh. *Quaker Organisation and Business Meetings.* London: Friends Home Service Committee, 1958.

Drayton, Brian. *Getting Rooted: Living in the Cross*, Pendle Hill Pamphlet #391. Wallingford, PA: Pendle Hill Publications, 2007.

—————. *On Living with a Concern for Gospel Ministry.* Philadelphia: QuakerPress of Friends General Conference, 2006.

Dymond, Jonathan. "Inquiry into the Accordancy of War with the Principles of Christianity" in Licia Kuenning, ed., *Historical Writings of Quakers against War.* Glenside, PA: Quaker Heritage Press, 2002.

Fager, Chuck. *Remaking Friends: How Progressive Friends Changed Quakerism and Helped Save America.* Durham, NC: Kimo Press, 2014.

Fell, Margaret. *The Life of Margaret Fox, Wife of George Fox, 1614-1702.* Philadelphia: Book Association of Friends, 1694, 1885. Available from the Digital Quaker Collection of Earlham School of Religion at http://esr.earlham.edu/dqc/.

Fell, Margaret. "Women's Speaking Justified." Available from Quaker Heritage Press at www.qhpress.org/texts/fell.html, 1666.

Fox, George, John L. Nickalls, ed. *The Journal of George Fox* (1694). Cambridge: Cambridge University Press, 1952.

—————. *Works*. Philadelphia: Marcus T. Gould, 1831.

Garman, Mary, Judith Applegate, Margaret Benefiel, and Dortha Meredith, eds. *Hidden in Plain Sight: Quaker Women's Writings 1650-1700*. Wallingford, PA: Pendle Hill Publications, 1996.

Gates, Thomas. *Members One of Another: The Dynamics of Membership in Quaker Meeting*, Pendle Hill Pamphlet #371. Wallingford, PA: Pendle Hill Publications, 2004.

Gwyn, Douglas. *Apocalypse of the Word: The Life and Message of George Fox*. Richmond, IN: Friends United Press. 1986.

—————. *The Covenant Crucified: Quakers and the Rise of Capitalism*. Wallingford, PA: Pendle Hill Publications, 1995.

—————. *Seekers Found: Atonement in Early Quaker Experience*. Wallingford, PA: Pendle Hill Publications, 2000.

—————. "Sense and Sensibilities: Quaker Bispirituality Today" in *Report from the Middle: Reflections on Divisions among Friends Today*. Boston, MA: Beacon Hill Friends House, 2005.

Hamm, Thomas. *The Transformation of American Quakerism: Orthodox Friends, 1800-1907*. Bloomington: Indiana University Press, 1992.

Hawken, Paul. *Blessed Unrest: How the Largest Social Movement in History Is Restoring Grace, Justice, and Beauty to the World*. New York: Penguin Books, 2007.

Heller, Michael, ed. *The Tendering Presence: Essays on John Woolman*. Wallingford, PA: Pendle Hill Publications, 2003.

Hinds, Hillary. *George Fox and Early Quaker Culture*. Manchester: Manchester University Press, 2011.

Ingle, H. Larry. *Quakers in Conflict: The Hicksite Reformation*. Knoxville: University of Tennessee Press, 1986.

Jones, Rufus M. "Introduction" to W. C. Braithwaite, *The Beginnings of Quakerism*. London: Macmillan, 1912.

Kelly, Thomas. *The Eternal Promise*. Richmond, IN: Friends United Press, 1966.

Kelly, Thomas. *A Testament of Devotion*. San Francisco: HarperCollins, 1941, 1992.

Kennedy, Thomas C. *British Quakerism 1860-1920: The Transformation of a Religious Community*. Oxford: Oxford University Press, 2001.

Loring, Patricia. *Listening Spirituality: vol. 1, Personal Spiritual Practices among Friends*. Washington: Openings Press, 1997.

—————. *Listening Spirituality, vol. II: Corporate Spiritual Practice among Friends*. Washington: Openings Press, 1999.

—————. *Spiritual Discernment: The Context and Goal of Clearness Committees*, Pendle Hill Pamphlet #305. Wallingford, PA: Pendle Hill Publications, 1992.

Lunn, Pam. *Costing Not Less Than Everything: Sustainability and Spirituality in Challenging Times*, 2011 Swarthmore Lecture. London: Quaker Books, 2011.

Marietta, Jack. *The Reformation of American Quakerism 1748-1783*. Philadelphia: University of Pennsylvania Press, 1984.

Marshall, Charles. *Journal*, London: Barett, 1844.

Mather, Eleanore Price. *Edward Hicks, Primitive Quaker: His Religion in Relation to His Art*, Pendle Hill Pamphlet #170. Wallingford, PA: Pendle Hill Publications, 1970.

McDaniel, Donna and Vanessa Julye. *Fit for Freedom, Not for Friendship: Quakers, African Americans, and the Myth of Racial Justice*. Philadelphia: QuakerPress of Friends General Conference, 2009.

Moore, Rosemary. *The Light in Their Consciences: Early Quakers in Britain 1646-1666*. University Park, PA: Pennsylvania State University, 2000.

Nayler, James. *Works*. Glenside, PA: Quaker Heritage Press, 2009.

Nicholson, Benjamin. *A Blast from the Lord*. 1653.

Penington, Isaac. *Some Directions to the Panting Soul* (1661) in *Works*, vol. 2. Glenside, PA: Quaker Heritage Press, 1994.

Penington, Mary. *Experiences in the Life of Mary Penington (Written by Herself)*. London: Headley, 1911.

Punshon, John. *Portrait in Grey: A Short History of the Quakers*, 2nd ed. London: Quaker Books, 2006.

—————. *Testimony and Tradition*, 1990 Swarthmore Lecture. London: London Yearly Meeting, 1990.

Sheeran, Michael J. *Beyond Majority Rule: Voteless Decisions in the Religious Society of Friends*. Philadelphia: Philadelphia Yearly Meeting, 1983, 1996.

Spencer, Carole. *Holiness: The Soul of Quakerism*. Notre Dame, IN: Paternoster Press, 2007.

Stephenson, Roy. *Freeing the Spirit: Nominations in the Society of Friends in Theory and Practice*. York: Sessions, 2009.

Stirredge, Elizabeth. *Strength in Weakness*. London, 1795.

Taber, Frances Irene. *Finding the Taproot of Simplicity: A Movement between Inner Knowledge and Outer Action*, Pendle Hill Pamphlet #400. Wallingford, PA: Pendle Hill Publications, 2009.

Taber, William. *Four Doors to Meeting for Worship*, Pendle Hill Pamphlet #306. Wallingford, PA: Pendle Hill Publications, 1992.

—————. Michael Birkel, ed. *The Mind of Christ: Bill Taber on the Meeting for Business*. Pendle Hill Pamphlet #406, Wallingford, PA: Pendle Hill Publications, 2010.

Wilson, Lloyd Lee. *Radical Hospitality*, Pendle Hill Pamphlet #427. Wallingford, PA: Pendle Hill Publications, 2014.

Wink, Walter. *Engaging the Powers: Discernment and Resistance in a World of Domination*. Philadelphia: Fortress Press, 1992.

—————. *The Human Being: Jesus and the Enigma of the Son of Man*. Philadelphia: Fortress Press, 2002.

Woolman, John, Phillips P. Moulton, ed. *The Journal and Major Essays of John Woolman*. New York: Oxford University Press, 1971.

Young, Mildred Binns. *Insured by Hope*, Pendle Hill Pamphlet #90. Wallingford, PA: Pendle Hill Publications, 1956.

ENDNOTES

Full citations for sources referenced below can be found above in Works Cited (p. 167).

PREFACE

1. For more information about Pendle Hill, see www.pendlehill.org.

INTRODUCTION

1. George Fox, *Journal*, John L. Nickalls, ed., pp. 1-2.
2. Ibid., p.2.
3. Bible quotations are from the New Revised Standard Version unless otherwise specified.
4. Fox, *Journal*, p. 3.
5. Ibid., pp. 9-10.
6. Ibid., pp. 11-12
7. Ibid., p. 12.
8. Ibid., pp. 14-15.
9. Ibid., p. 16.
10. Walter Wink, *The Human Being: Jesus and the Enigma of the Son of Man*, p. 27.
11. Fox, *Journal*, pp. 27-28.
12. Ibid., p. 27.
13. Ibid., p. 28.
14. Ibid., p. 22.
15. Ibid., pp. 33-34.
16. Ibid., pp. 36-37.
17. Ibid., p. 39.
18. Ibid., p. 104.

CHAPTER 1: *Quaker Spiritual Practice*

1. Margaret Fell, *The Life of Margaret Fox, Wife of George Fox*, p. 8.
2. Fox, *Journal*, p. 33.
3. Ibid., p. 19.
4. Quoted in Mary Garman, et al., *Hidden in Plain Sight*, p. 52.
5. Fox, *Works*, vol. 7, pp. 20-21.

6. Fox, *Journal*, p. 13.

7. Isaac Penington, "Some Directions to the Panting Soul" (1661) in *Works*, vol. 2, p. 205.

8. Thomas Kelly, *A Testament of Devotion*, pp. 3-4.

9. Ibid., p. 43.

10. Ibid., p. 47.

11. William Taber, *Four Doors to Meeting for Worship*, pp. 17-18.

12. Patricia Loring, *Listening Spirituality: vol. 1, Personal Spiritual Practices among Friends*, p. 2.

13. Hilary Hinds, *George Fox and Early Quaker Culture*, p. 118.

14. George Fox, quoted in Anne Adams, *Is There Not a New Creation?*, p. 28.

15. William Penn, *Some Fruits of Solitude*, quoted in Adams, p. 30.

16. Rex Ambler, *Light to Live By*, pp. 46-47.

17. Britain Yearly Meeting, *Quaker Faith & Practice* (1995), Chapter 1. All references to *Faith & Practice* refer to this edition, unless otherwise noted.

CHAPTER 2: *A Prophetic People*

1. Charles Marshall, quoted in Douglas Gwyn, *Seekers Found*, p. 253.

2. Francis Howgill, 1663, quoted in *Quaker Faith & Practice*, 19.08.

3. Rufus Jones, "Introduction" to W. C. Braithwaite, *The Beginnings of Quakerism*, p. xlii.

4. Fox, *Journal*, p. 123.

5. Fox, *Works*, vol. 4, pp. 17-18.

6. Taber, *Four Doors*, pp. 3-4.

7. Ibid., p. 5.

8. Ibid., p. 14.

9. Ibid., p. 16.

10. Fox, *Journal*, p. 346.

11. Taber, *Four Doors*, pp. 19-20.

12. Thomas Kelly, *The Eternal Promise*, p. 86.

13. Clarence Tucker Craig, in *The Interpreter's Bible*, vol. 10, p. 207.

14. Kelly, *Eternal Promise*, p. 102.

15. Lewis Benson, "On Being Moved by the Spirit to Minister in Public Worship" in *The Quaker Vision*, pp. 49-50.

16. Taber, *Four Doors*, pp. 25-26.

17. Kelly, *Eternal Promise*, p. 100.

18. Fox, *Works*, vol. 7, p. 19.

19. Fox, *Journal*, p. 175.

20. Benson, "On Being Moved by the Spirit to Minister in Public Worship," p. 49.

21. Caroline Steven (1908), quoted in *Quaker Faith & Practice*, 2.39.

22. Mary Penington, *Experiences in the Life of Mary Penington (Written by Herself)*, p. 45.

23. Kelly, *Eternal Promise*, pp. 102, 104-05.

CHAPTER 3: *"Mind the Oneness"*

1. Wilmer Cooper, *The Testimony of Integrity*, p. 6.
2. See, for example: Fox, *Journal*, p. 169.
3. John Conran, *Journal*, p. 26.
4. John Punshon, *Testimony and Tradition*, p. 94.
5. John Woolman, *Journal*, pp. 32-33.
6. Ibid., p. 51.
7. Ibid., p. 145.
8. Michael Birkel, *A Near Sympathy: The Timeless Quaker Wisdom of John Woolman*, p. 108.
9. Woolman, *Journal*, p. 28.
10. Ibid., pp. 247-48.
11. J. William Frost in Michael Heller, *The Tendering Presence*, pp. 167-89.
12. *Quaker Faith & Practice*, 13:1.
13. As this book goes to press, New England Yearly Meeting's 1985 Faith and Practice is under revision. The draft of Appendix 8, "Pastoral Care and Clearness Committees for Personal Discernment" (Jan. 30, 2014) can be accessed from: http://www.neym.org/fp-revision.
14. See Woolman, *Journal*, pp. 122-23.
15. Ibid., pp. 127-28.

CHAPTER 4: *Testimony in Conversation*

1. Fox, *Works*, vol. 6, p. 302.
2. Fox, *Journal*, p. 109.
3. Fox, *Works*, vol. 4, p. 109.
4. For the full text, see www.qhpress.org/texts/fell.html.
5. For more on Fox's "Fifty-Nine Particulars," see Douglas Gwyn, *The Covenant Crucified*, pp. 205-07.
6. Fox, *Journal*, p. 520.
7. Ibid., pp. 555-56.
8. Woolman, *Journal*, p. 241.
9. Ibid., p. 262.
10. Ibid., p. 236.
11. Ibid., p. 255.
12. From Britain Yearly Meeting, *Quaker Faith & Practice*, 23:16.
13. Ursula Franklin (1979), quoted in *Quaker Faith & Practice*, 23.32.

14. Emma Lapsansky, quoted in Donna McDaniel and Vanessa Julye, *Fit for Freedom, Not for Friendship*, p. 393.

CHAPTER 5: *The Peaceable Kingdom*

1. See Fox, *Journal*, p. 19.
2. Quoted in Eleanor Price Mather, *Edward Hicks*, p. 32.
3. Quoted in Britain Yearly Meeting, *Quaker Faith & Practice*, 2.87.
4. Britain Yearly Meeting, *Quaker Faith & Practice*, 3.02.
5. Howard Brinton, *Reaching Decisions*, p. 17.
6. Taber, *Mind of Christ*, pp. 17-19.
7. Ibid., p. 15.
8. Ibid., p. 8
9. Michael Sheeran, *Beyond Majority Rule*, pp. 53-54.
10. Ibid., pp. 81-82, 86-87.
11. Taber, *Mind of Christ*, p. 22.
12. For more on Quaker methods of group discernment, see Patricia Loring, *Listening Spirituality, vol. 2: Corporate Spiritual Practice among Friends*. For more on the membership in the meeting as a lifelong process, see Thomas Gates, *Members One of Another: The Dynamics of Membership in Quaker Meeting*.
13. Sheeran, *Beyond Majority Rule*, p. 103.
14. Douglas Steere, unpublished manuscript, quoted in Sheeran, *Beyond Majority Rule*, p. 91.
15. William Dewsbury, *The Faithful Testimony*, pp. 1-4, quoted in Douglas Gwyn, *Seekers Found*, pp. 307-08.
16. Bishop's letter is extensively quoted in Gwyn, *Seekers Found*, pp. 348-50.
17. Beatrice Saxon Snell, quoted in Britain Yearly Meeting, *Quaker Faith & Practice*, 12.8.
18. Two excellent sources on this traditional vocation of Friends ministry are Samuel Bownas's *A Description of the Qualifications Necessary to a Gospel Minister* and Brian Drayton's contemporary reflections, *On Living with a Concern for Gospel Ministry*.
19. For more about the meeting's discernment of gifts in leadership, see Roy Stephenson, *Freeing the Spirit: Nominations in the Society of Friends in Theory and Practice*.
20. See Andres Cornell, *Oppose and Propose!*, pp. 38-49.
21. William Erbury quoted in Braithwaite, *The Beginnings of Quakerism*, p. 570.

CHAPTER 6: *Tragedy and Renewal in Quaker History*

1. Helpful surveys of Quaker history include John Punshon, *Portrait in Grey*, and Hugh Barbour and J. William Frost, *The Quakers*.

2. For more on the radical ideas and groups that converged in the Quaker movement, see Gwyn, *Seekers Found*. For more on the apocalyptic message of George Fox, see Gwyn, *Apocalypse of the Word*. For more on early Quaker witness as a nonviolent anarchist revolution and its defeat, see Gwyn, *The Covenant Crucified*. For an excellent general introduction to early Friends, see Rosemary Moore, *The Light in Their Consciences*.

3. See John 3:19-22.

4. For more on the mixed accomplishments of this period, see Jack Marietta, *The Reformation of American Quakerism*.

5. For a good history of the Hicksite Separation, see H. Larry Ingle, *Quakers in Conflict*.

6. For more on changes among Orthodox Friends, see Thomas Hamm, *The Transformation of American Quakerism* and Carole Spencer, *Holiness: The Soul of Quakerism*. For more on Hicksite developments, see Thomas Hamm's forthcoming book on Hicksites in the nineteenth century and Chuck Fager's book on Progressive Quakers, *Remaking Friends*. For liberal developments among British Friends, see Thomas C. Kennedy, *British Quakers 1860-1920*.

7. Carole Spencer's book on Holiness, mentioned above, makes a positive case for that convergence.

8. Note Sheeran's *Beyond Majority Rule* as a specimen example of the emphasis upon clerkship. For a penetrating analysis of late twentieth-century British Friends, see Pink Dandelion, *A Sociological Analysis of the Theology of Quakers: The Silent Revolution*, 1996.

CHAPTER 7: *The Lamb's War*

1. Fox, *Works*, vol. 4, pp. 17-18.

2. See also Jeremiah 6:14.

3. For more on the early Quaker understanding of covenant, see Gwyn, *The Covenant Crucified*, pp. 6-7.

4. Benjamin Nicholson, *A Blast from the Lord*, pp. 10-11.

5. John Camm, *A Word from the Lord*, p. 4, quoted in Gwyn, *The Covenant Crucified*, pp. 149-50.

6. Fox, *Journal*, pp. 64-65.

7. Fox, *Works*, vol. 7, p. 20.

8. Walter Wink, *Engaging the Powers*, pp. 3-10.

9. Hugh Barbour and Arthur O. Roberts, *Early Quaker Writings*, p. 106.

10. Fox, *Journal*, p. 128.

11. James Nayler, *Works*, vol. 4, p. 382.

12. Woolman, *Journal*, p. 255.

13. Fox, *Journal*, p. 399.

14. Ibid., p. 402.

15. For more, see Peter Brock, *The Quaker Peace Testimony, 1660-1914*, pp. 75ff.

16. Jonathan Dymond, reprinted in Licia Kuenning, ed., *Historical Writings of Quakers Against War*.

17. Brock, *The Quaker Peace Testimony, 1660-1914*, pp. 257-64.

18. Britian Yearly Meeting, *Quaker Faith & Practice*, Chapter 24, Introduction.

CHAPTER 8: *Daily Delight*

1. Mildred Binns Young, *Insured by Hope*, pp. 7-11.

2. See also Luke 6:20-26.

3. This transformation of early Quakerism is traced in Gwyn, *The Covenant Crucified*.

4. For a good contemporary statement, see Lloyd Lee Wilson, *Radical Hospitality*.

5. I theorized this convergence under the rubric of "X-Covenant" in the Conclusion to Gwyn, *The Covenant Crucified*.

6. Charles Marshall, *Journal*, p. 3, quoted in Gwyn, *Seekers Found*, pp. 252-53.

7. Elizabeth Stirredge, *Strength in Weakness*, pp. 1-19, quoted in Gwyn, *Seekers Found*, p. 256.

8. Charles Marshall, "Testimony," in John Camm and John Audland, *The Memory of the Righteous Revived* (1689), quoted in Gwyn, *Seekers Found*, p. 255.

9. Francis Howgill (1663), quoted in Britain Yearly Meeting, *Quaker Faith & Practice*, 19:08.

10. Fox, *Journal*, pp. 205-06.

11. Fox, *Works*, vol. 7, p. 40.

12. Margaret Fell, 1700 manuscript, quoted in *Quaker Faith & Practice*, 20:31.

13. Woolman, *Journal*, pp. 239-40.

14. For more, see Adams, *Is There Not a New Creation?*, pp. 20-21.

15. Quoted in Paul Buckley, *The Essential Elias Hicks*, p. 17.

16. North Carolina Yearly Meeting (Conservative), *Faith and Practice*, 1983, p. 7.

17. Kelly, *Testament of Devotion*, pp. 91-95.

18. For another good contemporary Quaker treatment of simplicity, see Frances Irene Taber, *Finding the Taproot of Simplicity*.

19. For a cogent contemporary Quaker statement of the case, see Pam Lunn's 2011 Swarthmore Lecture, *Costing Not Less Than Everything*; also see the related Good Lives program at the Woodbrooke Quaker Study Centre: www.woodbrooke.org.uk/pages/good-lives.

20. Jonathan Dale, *Quaker Social Testimony*, p. 20.

21. Ibid., p. 26.

22. Ibid., pp. 27-28.

23. Audrey Urry, quoted in *Quaker Faith & Practice*, 25.04.

CONCLUSION: *The Sustainable Friends Meeting: Occupy!*

1. Walter Brueggemann, *The Land*, p. 5.

2. Chel Avery, in a private communication.

3. Thomas Gates, *Members One of Another*, p. 8.

4. See 1 John 4:18-19.

5. See Jim Corbett, *The Sanctuary Church and Goatwalking*.

6. Quoted in Hugh Doncaster, *Quaker Organisation and Business Meetings*, p. 43.

7. Brian Drayton's *On Living with a Concern for Gospel Ministry* describes well the spiritual formation of ministry in the manner of Friends, whatever expression it may take. Sandra Cronk's *Gospel Order* offers good material for group discussion, especially for meetings seeking to become more cohesive. Finally, William Taber's *Mind of Christ* is another good resource for meetings wishing to nurture deeper group discernment in meetings for business.

8. I describe the fruits of that experience in Douglas Gwyn, "Sense and Sensibilities: Quaker Bispirituality Today."

9. For a good contemporary statement of that synthesis, see Brian Drayton's "Letter to Friends" on "Why Climate Change is a Spiritual Challenge" in *Befriending Creation*, November-December 2011, published by Quaker Earthcare Witness (http://www.quakerearthcare.org).

10. Fox, Epistle #227, *Works*, vol. 7, p. 241.

CPSIA information can be obtained
at www.ICGtesting.com
Printed in the USA
BVOW09s0155040617
485947BV00001B/6/P